Raising Cane

The Unexpected Martial Art

Octavio Ramos Jr.

velluminous

Published by Velluminous Press
www.velluminous.com

ISBN-13: 978-1-905605-10-1
ISBN-10: 1-905605-10-2

cover illustration by Elspeth Fahey

Raising Cane

For my girls
Christine, Teresa, and Gloria

Contents

Part One
Basics

Introduction

When you think of a cane, do you imagine an elderly person walking down the street, using the 'stick' as a crutch? Do you picture an injured or handicapped individual slowly making his or her way down a grocery store aisle? Does the mere sight of a cane signal weakness and vulnerability?

When I think of a cane, I see a hard-hitting stick with a crook and horn capable of incapacitating any assailant in a matter of seconds. I see the most incredible self-defense tool ever created.

After years of studying Kali (a Filipino stick-fighting martial art also known as Escrima or Arnis de Mano), I discovered the Goju-Shorei Weapons Branch, founded by Master David McNeill. This martial arts system uses only street-legal weapons, such as the cane, the folding knife, and the fan.

I studied the cane and found it the most modern, versatile, and law-abiding weapon ever created.

The cane can be used as a stick, but it also has a curved crook and a horn that easily can trap an opponent's neck, arms, ribs, or legs. It can be carried anywhere and it will never attract undue attention. I know this from personal experience—I have even carried my cane through airport security without so much as a raised eyebrow.

After studying this unique weapon, I felt compelled to write a book that chronicles an all-inclusive system dedicated to self-defense with a cane. The result of this effort is what you hold in your hands.

I have incorporated many Filipino stick-fighting techniques into each of the book's sections, but these in no way detract from the Goju-Shorei system. Like the legendary Bruce Lee, I am a strong supporter of mixing a variety of martial arts styles.

I believe the combination of techniques presented herein serves as a strong foundation for effective self-protection.

In addition to Master McNeill, I am indebted to Master Mark Shuey, the man behind CaneMasters. CaneMasters creates fighting canes—and I mean *fighting canes.*

I own a plain walking cane (known as the Guardian Cane), as well as a custom job designed for effective self-protection. Information about CaneMasters can be found at the end of this introduction.

As with any martial art, make sure you are in good physical condition before practicing any of these techniques. In particular, make sure your joints can tolerate the stresses of handling and manipulating the cane. If you are unsure of your physical condition, you should consult a physician first.

Important!

Understand that this is a self-defense system and should never be used to inflict harm upon others. Just as importantly, recognize your limitations and never stand your ground if there is an avenue of escape. What does this mean? Run, run, and run. Only if you are cornered or have no other recourse, should you fight, fight, fight.

To learn more about CaneMasters, please call 1-800-422-CANE or visit their Web site at *www.canemasters.com*.

If you require more information about the Goju-Shorei Weapons Branch, please send an e-mail to *dave_goju@pyramid.net* or visit the master's Web site at *www.gojushorei.com*.

Cane Nomenclature

Think of a cane as a stick with teeth. The 'stick' component consists of the shaft and tip, whereas the 'teeth' component consists of the crook and horn (Fig. 1). The stick component can be used to thrust (using the tip), strike (using the end of the shaft), and block all types of attack. It is the crook, however, where the cane can generate its most effective (and devastating) maneuvers.

A stylist can use the crook and horn to take down an opponent by an arm or a leg—or even worse, to take down an assailant by the neck. The horn can be buried into a groin, ribs, or other soft body parts. A simple pull on the shaft and the opponent will be in agony, which will in many cases lead to incapacitation. Defensively, the crook and horn can be used to disarm an opponent.

Specially designed canes offer additional self-defense options. For example, some canes have a sharpened horn, which enables a stylist to more easily penetrate an opponent's soft areas. Canes can also have 'bumps' along the crook or shaft; such protrusions can cause damage when a stylist strikes or 'rubs' the cane on a soft spot or along bone.

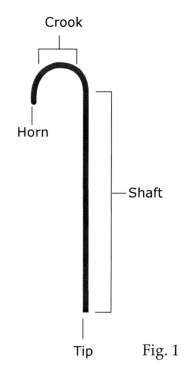

Fig. 1

Strong and Weak Sides

To help you learn the techniques contained in this book, I have divided the body in half (Fig. 2). The half that holds the cane is called the strong side, with the other half known as the weak side. It does not matter if your are left- or right-hand dominant.

To truly master these techniques, you must practice them using either hand effectively. The hand wielding the cane is known as the weapon hand; the empty hand is called the Alive Hand (in some systems it is also considered the supplemental-weapon hand). The Alive Hand can be used to block or check an opponent's attack, or if it also has a supplemental weapon it can be used to mount a secondary, or follow-up, attack.

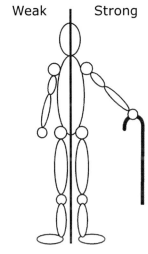

Fig. 2

Alive-Hand Placement

The principal purpose of the Alive Hand is to protect the heart. Thus, the hand rests on the chest, with the elbow tucked into the rib cage (Fig. 3). The idea is to sacrifice your hand before exposing your heart.

Some Filipino stick-fighting systems call the Alive Hand the Sacrifice Hand for this reason. Another possible reason for this placement is for economy of motion. In other words, the hand does not interfere with the dominant hand's movement and the entire arm itself presents a minimal target. Many Filipino fighting systems advocate a 'taking anything presented to you' style, and thus keeping the Alive Hand a minimal target ensures that it is not unduly sacrificed.

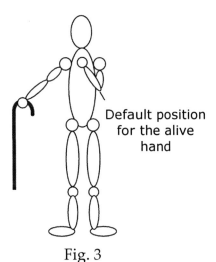

Fig. 3

Perpetual Blows

Once you have learned the techniques outlined in this book, you should practice combining them until you have developed a flow between strikes, blocks, takedowns, disarms, and other techniques.

This self-defense method advocates that you continue to strike until an opponent is down on the ground. Inflict as many blows as possible, using all the strength in your body to execute each strike.

In the heat of combat, you will strike blindly, with the majority of blows missing the target. That is why you should continue to strike—eventually, the cane will connect.

As you mature as a stylist, you most likely will remain calm during a fight, thus enabling you to strike more accurately at an opponent's vital areas. Or better yet, you will "take out" anything your opponent does not defend, such as a finger, a knee, a chin, until he or she is in so much pain that you can move in and inflict damage on even more vulnerable areas.

The key to winning a fight is to move ever-forward, invading the opponent's space, all the while striking as much as possible with as much power as possible.

Stances

Martial arts are filled with proper stances; this system will address the three most basic and effective of them, particularly as they pertain to the cane. Based on fencing and stick-fighting methods, these stances will enable you to move forward when attacking and to move backward when defending.

The sets at the end of Parts Two and Three will incorporate these stances and will demonstrate how to advance and retreat with them. Before you begin to practice these stances, make sure you understand which half of your body you consider the strong side and which you consider the weak side.

Strong Stance

To assume this stance, bring your strong foot forward so that it is approximately 45° from your weak foot (Fig. 4). You can place a stick on the floor diagonally to ensure that both feet line up properly (Fig. 5).

Your weapon hand should hold the cane upward, ready to strike or defend at any moment. The Alive Hand should be in its default position, protecting the heart (or holding a secondary weapon at the ready).

Weak Stance

To assume this stance, bring your strong foot back so that it is approximately 45° from your weak foot (Fig. 6). Use a stick to make sure you are in proper position (Fig. 7). Weapon and Alive hands remain the same.

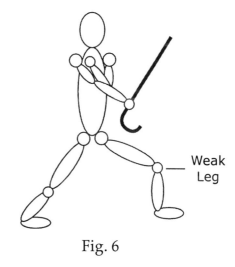

Fig. 6

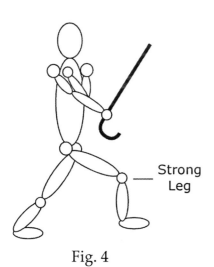

Fig. 4

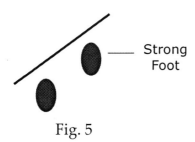

Fig. 5

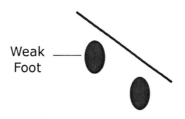

Fig. 7

Neutral Stance

The neutral stance is perhaps the stance you will take when on the street (Fig. 8). This stance serves as an intermediate step between the strong and the weak stances. From this stance you can assume either position at a moment's notice.

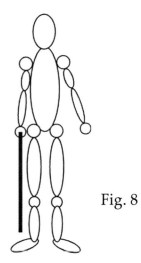

Fig. 8

Footwork

The three basic stances outlined in the previous section lead to a triangular style of movement. Triangle principles are very common in Filipino stick-fighting techniques. This basic system of footwork will enable you to move quickly and dodge all types of attacks. It also will enable you to strike from a number of angles.

Triangle Principle

Note: the following descriptions and figures assume that the strong side of your body is your right hand side. If this is not the case, the positions of '1' and '2' in the figures will be reversed.

To try out the triangle principle, place two sticks in the shape of a 'V' on the floor and stand at the closed end of the 'V' (Fig. 9). Assume a strong stance by moving your strong foot to the end of the stick labeled '2' (Fig. 10).

From this position, you can shift into a neutral stance. To do this, bring the weak foot forward so that it is next to the end of the stick labeled '1' (Fig. 11).

Fig. 9

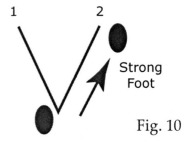

Strong Foot

Fig. 10

From this position, you can move into a weak stance. To do this, bring the strong foot back to where both sticks meet (Fig. 12).

Reverse the steps and go from a weak stance all the way to closure, where both feet are at the point at which the sticks intersect. As you become comfortable with this movement, pivot in another direction and make even more triangles.

To pivot, use the foot that has more weight on it. Turn this foot 90° either to the left or to the right. Create a full triangle and pivot again. If you pivot four times clockwise or counterclockwise, you will face all four geographical directions (north, south, east, and west). You also can pivot at another angle, thus creating yet another angle of attack.

Your pivot foot can be used to confront multiple attackers. As you defend against and subsequently dispatch one attacker, you then can pivot and face another.

As you become accustomed to these movements, you can begin to manipulate your entire body. For example, you can crouch, strike low then high, alternate your strong and weak sides, bring the cane around your back, and so on.

Combining such movements with speed will often confuse your opponent because in effect your can create unlimited angles of attack.

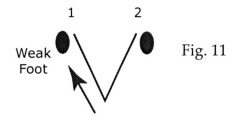

Fig. 11

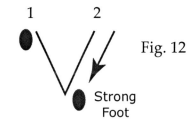

Fig. 12

Part Two
Strikes

Power Strikes

Power consists of force coupled with speed. Regardless of the stick-fighting system, there are in essence nine strikes designed to deliver maximum power. This section presents these strikes.

Some Filipino systems call the two sets the *Cinco Tiros,* which is Spanish for the 'Five Shots' or 'Five Blows.' There are two sets of *Cinco Tiros,* both of which have one strike (the thrust) in common.

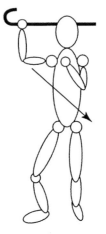

Fig. 13

How do you know if your strikes are generating power? Each strike must literally 'break wind.' As you execute a strike, listen for a whoosh-like sound. That sound means you are beginning to generate power. Unless otherwise noted, the Alive Hand should be kept in the default position during these strikes.

At the end of each *Cinco Tiros* set, I have provided a full graphical representation of the strike-flow pattern.

Power Strike One: Sweep Down

Assume a strong stance. Bring your weapon arm up, folding the elbow so that your forearm is parallel with the body and the cane is perpendicular to it (Fig. 13).

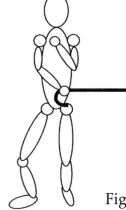

Fig. 14

With as much force and speed as possible, sweep the cane downward, with the shaft coming from your strong side to your weak side (see the arrow on Fig. 13).

The cane's momentum should carry it around your waistline (Fig. 14). Because of the power you are generating, let the cane wrap around your weak hip (Fig. 15). This will enable you to stop to the cane's momentum without sacrificing power.

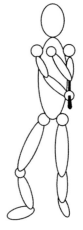

Fig. 15

Power Strike Two: Sweep Up

To execute this strike, simply reverse the steps outlined in Power Strike One (as shown in figs. 16-18). To generate additional power, you can use the Alive Hand to "push off" from the cane's shaft.

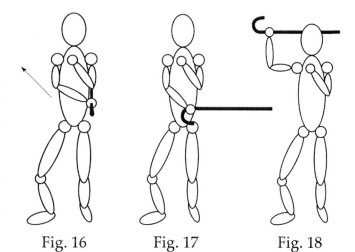

Fig. 16   Fig. 17   Fig. 18

Power Strike Three: Reverse Sweep Up

With the cane perpendicular to your body from having finished Power Strike Two (Fig. 18), bring the cane down so that it parallels your body (Fig. 19). Continue the movement downward until the shaft is perpendicular to your shoulder and hip (Fig. 20).

Once you complete this preparatory move, muster all the power you can and swing the cane to your weak shoulder (Fig. 21).

Use your own body to stop the cane's momentum (Fig. 22).

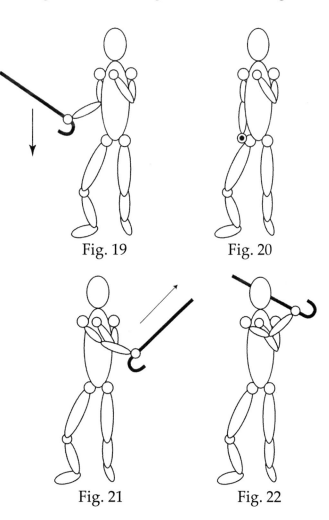

Fig. 19   Fig. 20

Fig. 21   Fig. 22

Power Strike Four: Reverse Sweep Down

To execute this strike, reverse the steps from Power Strike Three (as shown in figs. 23-25). You can use the Alive Hand to generate more power by pushing off from the cane's shaft.

Power Strike Five: Forward Thrust

With the cane perpendicular to your hip (as in Fig. 25 and shown side view on Fig. 26 below), extend your weapon hand forward, thrusting the cane's tip into an opponent (Fig. 27). Thrust high or low.

Fig. 23

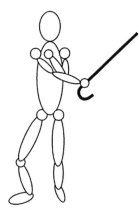

Fig. 24

Fig. 25

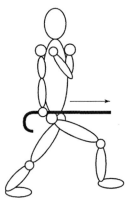

Fig. 26

Fig. 27

Set One: Cinco Tiros

The page opposite shows how you can practice all five strikes in unison. Practice this set to develop a fluidity of movement between strikes. However, remember to use as much force and speed as possible to execute each blow.

Set One of the Cinco Tiros resembles a multiplication sign (or an "X") in its movement and is thus sometimes referred to as the "X" exercise.

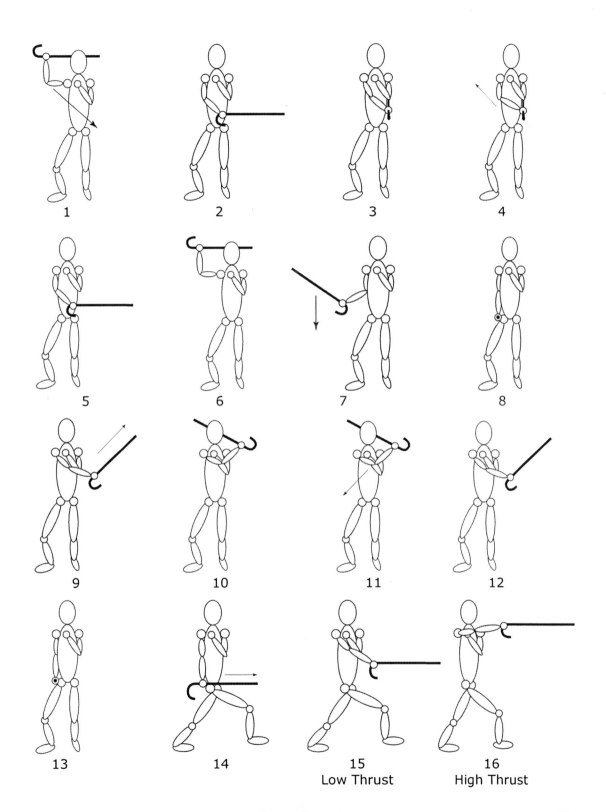

1

2

3

4

5

6

7

8

9

10

11

12

13

14

15
Low Thrust

16
High Thrust

Power Strike Six: Horizontal Sweep

Assume a strong stance and hold the cane parallel with your body (Fig. 28). Bring the cane's tip down by moving your wrist slightly clockwise (Fig. 29). As soon as the cane is perpendicular to your body, horizontally sweep the cane across from your strong side to your weak side, with the shaft pointing away from your strong side (Fig. 30). The swing can be low (as shown) or high (across your face).

Generate as much power as possible, using your own body to stop the cane's momentum (Fig. 31). Use your hips to generate even more force; as you execute this strike with your hips, the momentum should cause you to twist slightly. Make sure to maintain balance while generating maximum power.

Power Strike Seven: Reverse Horizontal Sweep

To execute this strike, simply reverse the steps discussed in Power Strike Six (as shown in figs. 32-34). To generate additional power, you can use the Alive Hand to push off from the cane's shaft.

Figure 34 shows the cane at the end of the movement. The cane's momentum is stopped by your wrist and elbow, and thus the cane should be perpendicular to your body but parallel with your shoulders.

Before executing the next power strike, point the cane's tip outward (Fig. 35). This step will prepare you for the next power strike. Again, you can swing low (midsection) or high (face).

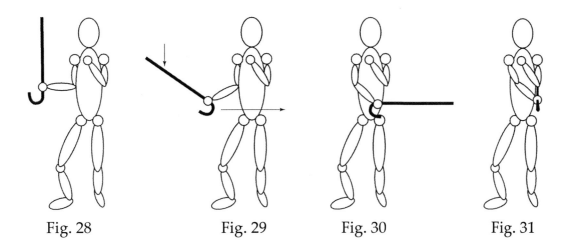

Fig. 28   Fig. 29   Fig. 30   Fig. 31

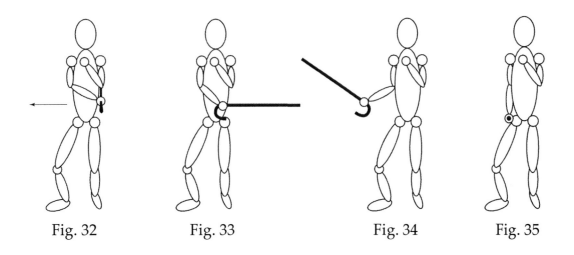

Fig. 32   Fig. 33   Fig. 34   Fig. 35

Power Strike Eight: Vertical Up

Having pointed the cane's tip outward while it is on your hip (Fig. 36), bring the cane upward (Fig. 37) until the elbow is locked into a straight position (Fig. 38). To execute this strike with maximum power, think of the following: Imagine you have stuck the cane's tip into the ground. Pull the stick out at an angle (like a shovel, only you are using one hand), as if you are throwing dirt into the air.

Power Strike Nine: Vertical Down

To execute this strike, simply reverse the steps outlined in Power Strike Eight (as shown in figs. 39-40). To generate additional power, you can use the Alive Hand to push off from the cane's shaft. Figure 40 shows the cane at the end of this strike's movement. The cane's momentum is stopped by your wrist and elbow, and thus the cane is perpendicular to your body but parallel with your shoulders.

Power Strike Ten: Forward Thrust

With the cane perpendicular to your hip (Fig. 41 shows a side view), extend the weapon hand, thrusting the cane's tip into an opponent (Fig. 42). Thrust high or low.

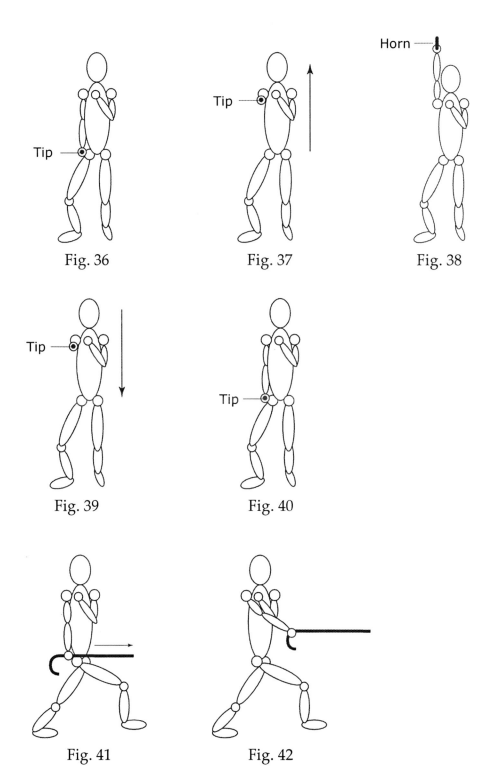

Fig. 36

Fig. 37

Fig. 38

Fig. 39

Fig. 40

Fig. 41

Fig. 42

Set Two: Cinco Tiros

The page opposite shows how you can practice all five strikes of Set Two. Practice this set to develop fluidity of movement between strikes, while remembering to use as much force and speed as possible to execute each strike.

Set Two of the Cinco Tiros resembles an addition sign or a cross in its movements.

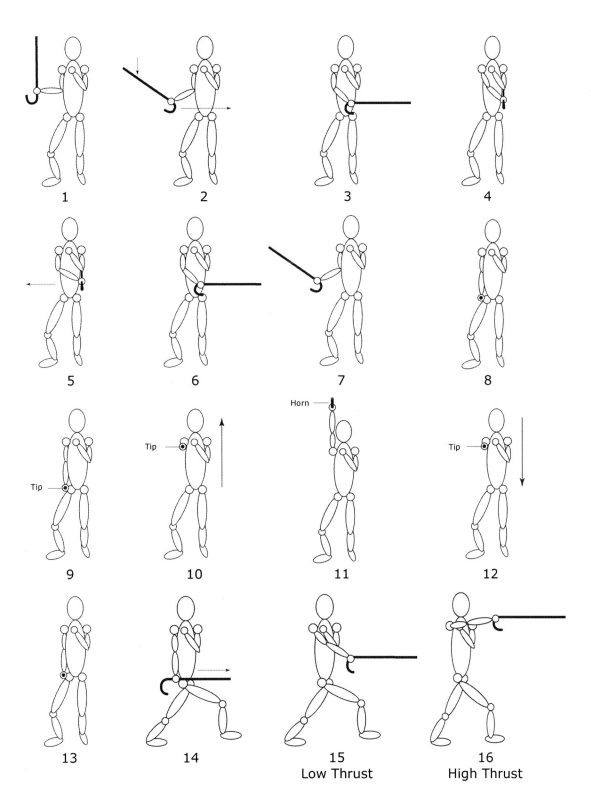

1

2

3

4

5

6

7

8

9

Tip

10

Tip

11

Horn

12

Tip

13

14

15
Low Thrust

16
High Thrust

Flexibility Strikes

Some of the fancier strikes with the cane are achieved by using the wrist and forearm. These spinning techniques require both strength and flexibility.

There are two fundamental flexibility strikes: the Figure Eight "X" and the Figure Eight Arrow. These techniques consist of two fundamental spinning moves, which in the Filipino arts are known as *Redondos* (Spanish for "circles").

Strong-Side Redondos

Begin by holding the cane with its tip upward. Assume a strong stance (Fig. 43 opposite). Using your wrist, turn the cane in a small circle around the strong side of your body (figs. 44-46). You complete the technique by returning to the original position (Fig. 43).

Make sure to keep your fingers wrapped around the cane's shaft. Do not release or relax them. Such a habit is dangerous. You may lose your weapon if someone strikes at your cane and your fingers are not completely wrapped around it as you perform this technique.

Strong-Side Reverse Redondo

To execute this technique, simply reverse the Strong-Side Redondo (see figs. 47-50 opposite). This technique may take a little more time to execute with some proficiency, but work on it and never relax your grip. If you relax your grip, an opponent could strike at the cane as you spin it; a loose grip means that the cane may be "slapped" out of your hand.

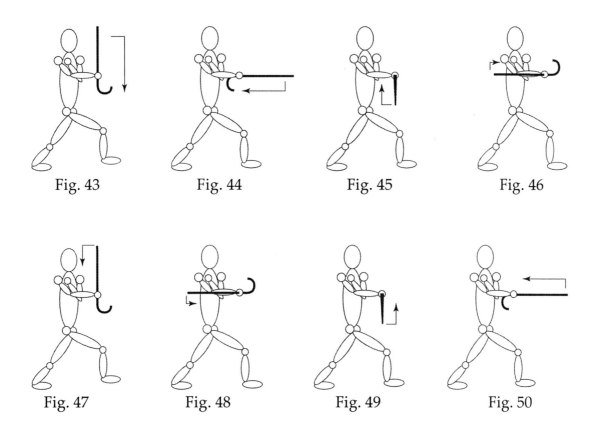

Fig. 43   Fig. 44   Fig. 45   Fig. 46

Fig. 47   Fig. 48   Fig. 49   Fig. 50

Weak-Side Redondo

Begin by holding the cane with its tip upward. Assume a strong stance (Fig. 51 opposite). Using your wrist, turn the cane in a small circle around the weak side of your body (see fig. 52-54). You complete the technique by returning to the original position (Fig. 51).

Weak-Side Reverse Redondo

To execute this technique, simply reverse the Weak-Side Redondo (as shown in figs. 55-58 opposite).

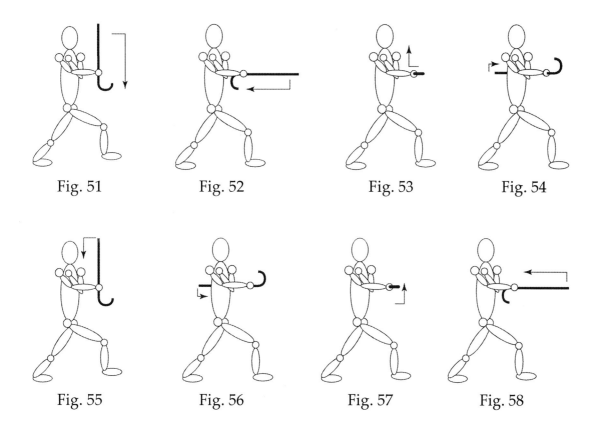

Fig. 51

Fig. 52

Fig. 53

Fig. 54

Fig. 55

Fig. 56

Fig. 57

Fig. 58

Figure Eight: The "X"

This figure eight pattern (shown below) consists of a Strong-Side Redondo followed by a Weak-Side Redondo. When executing this technique, keep your arm as stationary as possible. Let the wrist do the majority of the work.

As you become comfortable with this maneuver, pick up the pace and "flick" the wrist to generate even more power. As you go from one redondo to another, you should begin to see an "X" form across your body.

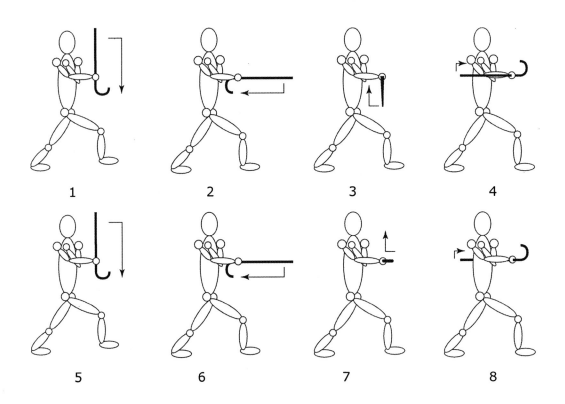

1   2   3   4

5   6   7   8

Figure Eight: The Arrow

This figure eight pattern (shown below) consists of a Weak-Side Reverse Redondo followed up by a Strong-Side Reverse Redondo. As you go from one redondo to another, you should begin to see an arrow form across your body.

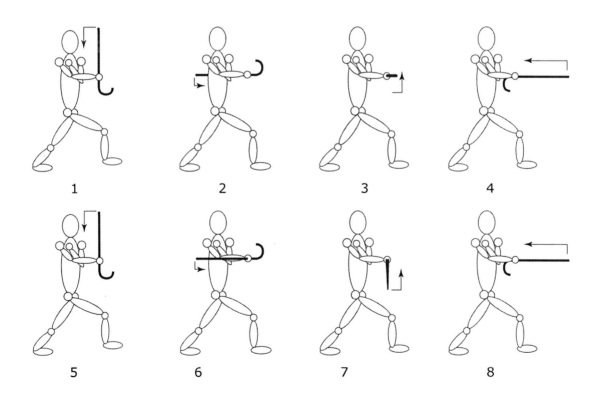

1

2

3

4

5

6

7

8

Strike Set and Flow

This section presents thirteen basic strikes. This set is part of the training necessary to obtain a yellow belt in the Goju-Shorei Weapons Branch. Practice these techniques with your left and right arm so that both can gain equal proficiency.

Strong-Side Low-Level Strike

Technique
Assume a neutral stance and hold the cane with your thumb pointing downward (Fig. 59 opposite). Moving the strong foot forward, bring the cane around your weak side in a circular motion—the tip points toward your weak side (Fig. 60). Once your thumb is parallel with your forearm (Fig. 61), bring the arm and shoulder toward your weak side (Fig. 62).

Strike the target with the end of the shaft (note the strike zone shown on Fig. 62). Remember to carry the strike all the way through—do not stop until the cane is literally wrapped around the weak side of your body (Fig. 63). Use your hips and lateral muscles to generate additional power.

You may wish to crouch when executing a low strike (particularly if you are going for an opponent's ankle). Instead of bending your back (which can expose your head and neck), slightly fold your calves into your thighs (Fig. 64). Focus on the opponent's movements, not on the strike areas.

Strike Areas

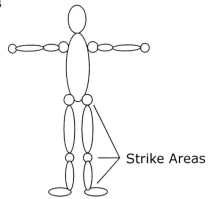

Strike Areas

Alive Hand
The Alive Hand can help protect you from any blows that come in while you are in the crouching position (Fig. 65).

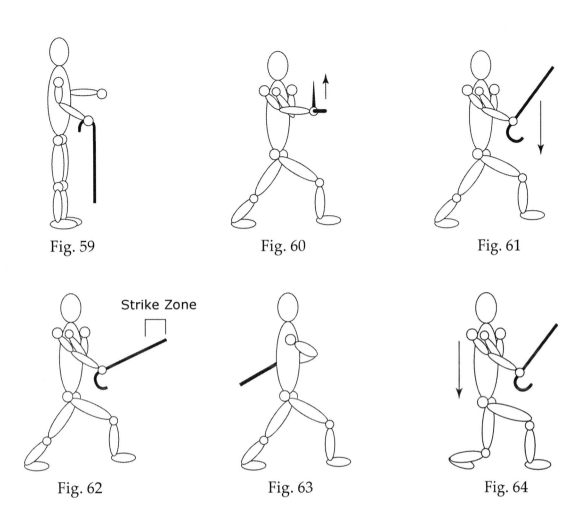

Fig. 59   Fig. 60   Fig. 61

Strike Zone

Fig. 62   Fig. 63   Fig. 64

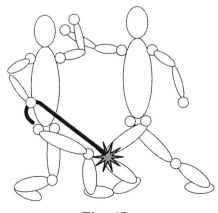

Fig. 65

Weak-Side Low-Level Strike

Technique

This strike is similar to the Strong-Side Low-Level Strike, only it targets the opponent's other side.

Hold the cane as before (see Fig. 66 opposite). Moving the weak foot forward, bring the cane around your strong side (the tip points toward your strong side) in a circular motion (Fig. 67).

Once your thumb is parallel with your forearm (Fig. 68), bring the arm and shoulder toward your strong side (Fig. 69), striking the target. Use your hips and lateral muscles to generate power.

Remember to carry the strike completely through the motion. Your wrist will be in an awkward position (palm facing the strong side), so you may want to practice this strike on a heavy bag to develop optimum power.

Strike Areas

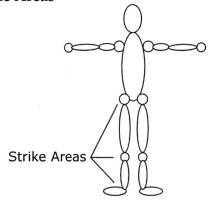

Strike Areas

Alive Hand

The Alive Hand should remain close to the heart during this strike, ready for any supplemental move. For example, if an attacker bends down slightly to block the cane's blow, you might use the Alive Hand to reach out and either:

- grab your opponent's hair (and follow up with a knee strike) or
- use your fingers to damage any of the attacker's senses, such as the eyes or nose.

Fig. 66

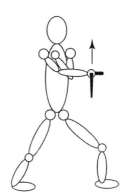

Fig. 67

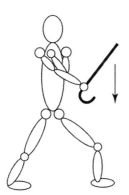

Fig. 68

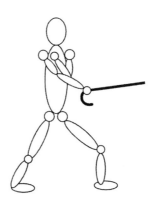

Fig. 69

Weak-Side Groin Thrust

Technique

From the starting position (see Fig. 70 opposite), move your weak foot forward and at the same time bend your elbow so that the cane's tip points upward (Fig. 71).

After dropping your arm slightly to bend the cane at a slight angle (Fig. 72), drive the cane into the opponent's groin area, using the horn to hook the opponent's pelvic area near the tailbone (Fig. 73). Bring the strong foot forward the pull the cane up (Fig. 74).

Strike Area

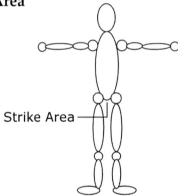

Strike Area

Alive Hand

The Alive Hand can be used to pull up the cane with extra force (Fig. 74).

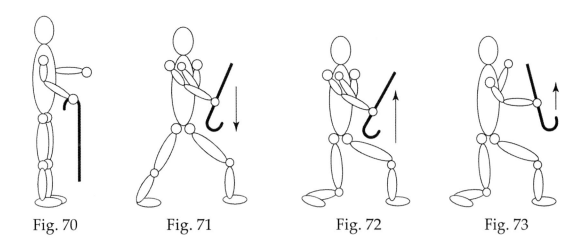

Fig. 70   Fig. 71   Fig. 72   Fig. 73

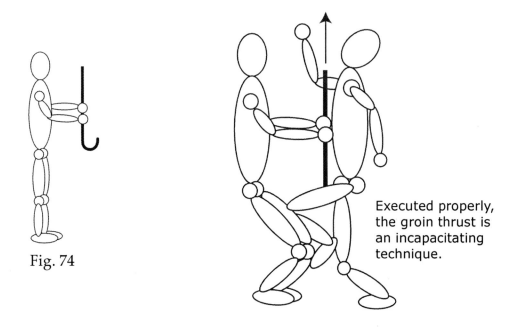

Fig. 74

Executed properly,
the groin thrust is
an incapacitating
technique.

Weak-Side Low-Level Thrust

Technique

This technique is similar to one used in fencing. From the starting position (see Fig. 75 opposite), move your weak foot forward and bend your elbow, thus bringing the cane's tip upward (Fig. 76). Bring your arm back into the side of your body (as if you were going to throw a punch) and lower the cane to the target area (Fig. 77).

Extend the arm forward, thrusting the cane's tip into your opponent (Fig. 78). Use your shoulders, back, and hips to generate power.

A thrust maneuver forces your opponent to step back (thus creating distance) or to one side (at which time you can follow up with another technique).

Use a thrust at close to medium range. Do not overextend yourself because the cane and your arm can easily become targets.

Strike Areas

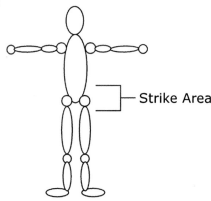

Strike Area

Alive Hand

The Alive Hand can be used to protect the weak side of the body from any blows. You also can use it to help thrust the cane into an opponent's body.

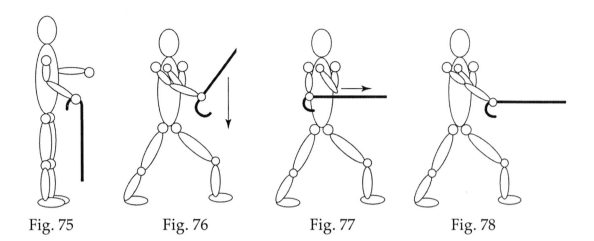

Fig. 75   Fig. 76   Fig. 77   Fig. 78

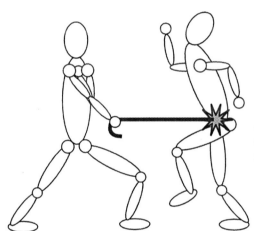

A thrust to the groin
or gut is extremely
effective

Do not overextend
yourself. Your
opponent can seize
an opening and
counterstrike so that
you may even lose
your weapon.

Strong-Side Mid-Level Strike

Technique

Hold the cane with your thumb pointing downward (see Fig. 79 opposite). Moving the strong foot forward, bring the cane around your weak side in a circular motion—the tip points toward your weak side (Fig. 80). Once your thumb parallels your forearm, bring the arm and shoulders toward your weak side (Fig. 81).

Strike the target within the cane's most effective strike zone (see Fig. 81). Remember to carry the strike all the way through—do not stop until the cane is literally wrapped around the weak side of your body (Fig. 82). Use your hips and lateral muscles to generate additional power.

Strike Areas

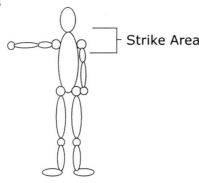

Strike Area

Alive Hand

The Alive Hand can help protect you from any blows that come in while you are executing the strike (Fig. 83). This figure also shows how a mid-level strike can be used to disarm an opponent. The hand is an extremely important target for the edge of the cane's shaft. A disarmed opponent is less likely to continue a fight.

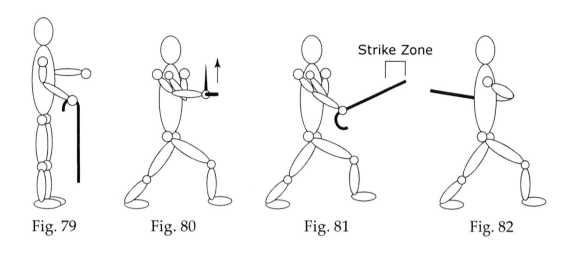

Fig. 79   Fig. 80   Fig. 81   Fig. 82

Strike Zone

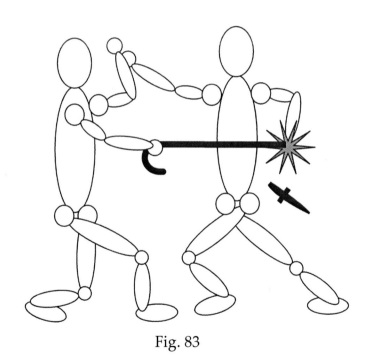

Fig. 83

Weak-Side Mid-Level Strike

Technique

This strike is similar to the Strong-Side Mid-Level Strike, only it targets the opponent's other side.

Hold the cane as before (see Fig. 84 opposite). Moving the weak foot forward, bring the cane around your strong side (the tip points toward your strong side) in a circular motion (Fig. 85). Once your thumb is parallel with your forearm (Fig. 86), bring the arm and shoulder toward your strong side (Fig. 87). Use your hips and lateral muscles to generate power.

Remember to carry the strike completely through the motion. Your wrist will be in an awkward position (palm facing the strong side and the blade of your hand parallel with your shoulder), so you may want to practice this strike on a heavy bag to develop power.

Strike Areas

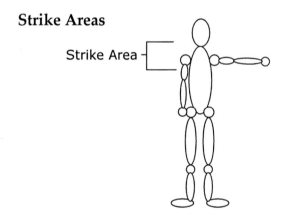

Strike Area

Alive Hand

The Alive Hand should remain close to the heart during this strike.

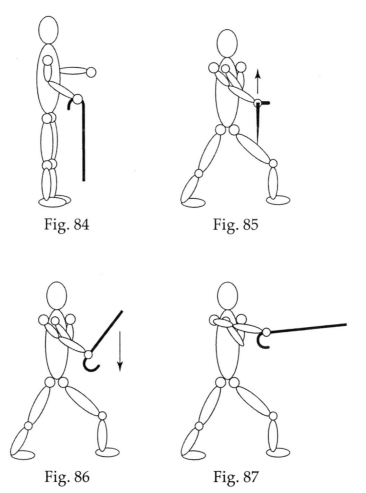

Fig. 84

Fig. 85

Fig. 86

Fig. 87

Weak-Side Thrust

Technique

From the starting position (see Fig. 88 opposite), move your weak foot forward and bend your elbow, thus bringing the cane's tip upward (Fig. 89). Bring your arm back into the side of your body (as if you were going to throw a punch) and prepare to thrust (Fig. 90).

Extend the arm forward, thrusting the cane's tip into your opponent (Fig. 91). Use your shoulders, back, and hips to generate power.

Preferred targets include the diaphragm (the bottom center of the rib cage), collarbone, or the base of the neck (especially the soft section of the throat). A thrust to the head could be very effective, but remember that it is an easy target to miss.

Use a thrust at close or medium range. Do not overextend yourself because the cane and your arm can easily become targets.

Strike Areas

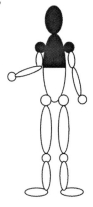

Alive Hand

The Alive Hand can be used to protect the weak side of the body from any blows. You also can use it to help thrust the cane into an opponent's body.

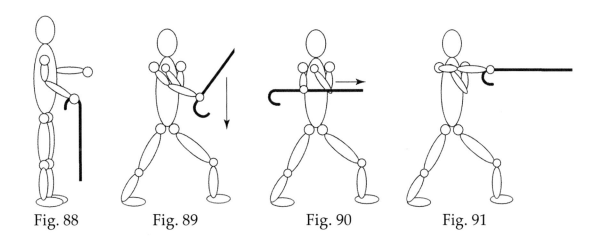

Fig. 88   Fig. 89   Fig. 90   Fig. 91

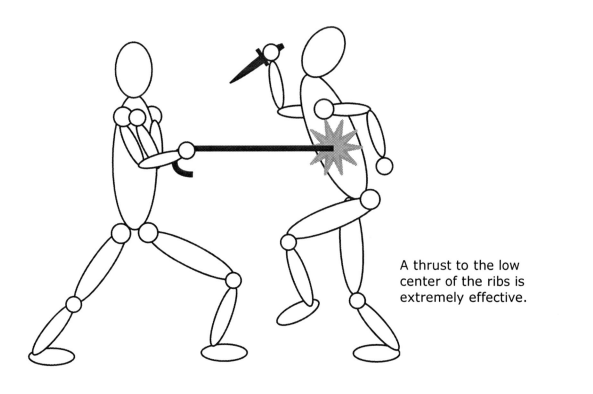

A thrust to the low
center of the ribs is
extremely effective.

Weak-Side Neck Grab

Technique

This technique is extremely dangerous to your assailant.

From the neutral stance (see Fig. 92 opposite), shift into a weak stance but leave the cane's tip pointed down. Bring the cane up and wrap the crook around an opponent's neck (Fig. 93). Once the crook is around the neck (Fig. 94), generate as much force as you can muster and bring the cane down at an angle, ending in the position shown in Fig. 95.

Once you have control of the opponent, you can execute a number of follow-up techniques. The traditional technique is to follow up with an elbow strike from the Alive Hand (Fig. 96).

Other possible techniques include a knee strike to the midsection or chest; a knee strike to the face, a come-along to the ground, or a come-along to a choke position. Figures 97 and 98 demonstrate a knee to the midsection. A come-along to a choke position is demonstrated for the next strike, which is a mirror image of this one.

Strike Area

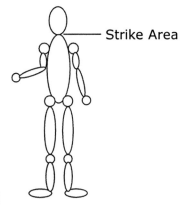

Alive Hand

The Alive Hand remains in the default position. It can be used to strike once the cane is wrapped around an opponent's neck (as shown in Fig. 96) or it can be used to reinforce the hold on the cane while executing a knee or come-along technique.

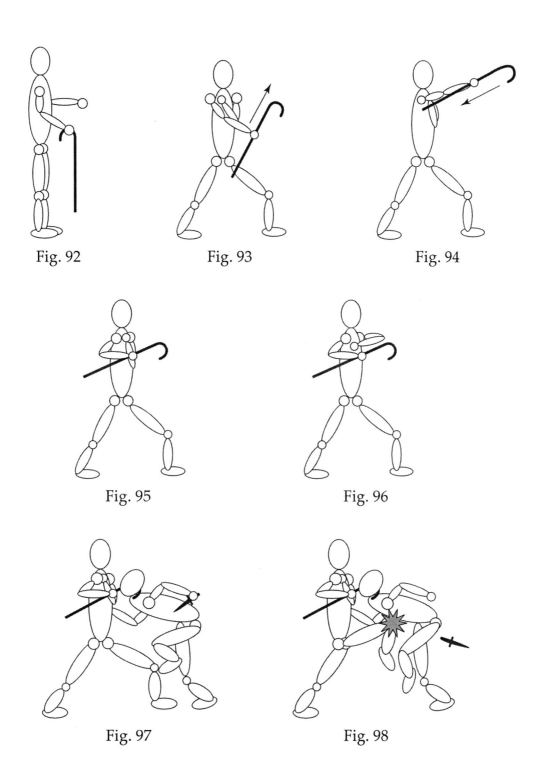

Fig. 92

Fig. 93

Fig. 94

Fig. 95

Fig. 96

Fig. 97

Fig. 98

Strong-Side Neck Grab

Technique

This is the mirror image of the Weak-Side Neck Grab. From the neutral stance (see Fig. 99 opposite), shift into a strong stance but leave the cane's tip pointed down. Bring the cane up and wrap the crook around an opponent's neck (Fig. 100). Once the crook is around the neck (Fig. 101), generate as much force as you can muster and bring the cane down at an angle, ending in the position shown in Fig. 102.

Once you have control of an opponent, you can execute a number of follow-up techniques. The traditional technique is to follow up with a palm-heel strike from the Alive Hand (Fig. 103). This type of martial art strike involves using the heel of the palm to strike vital areas in the face, particularly the nose or the windpipe along the neck.

Once your hand strikes the face, the fingers can be used to "rake" down the eyes and cheeks. In some Chinese systems, this is called the dragon's claw or tiger's paw.

Figures 104-106 demonstrate a come-along switched to a choke hold position. After wrapping an opponent's neck with the cane, step forward, making sure the cane remains around the opponent's neck. Once your are back-to-back, you can pull down on the shaft.

Strike Area

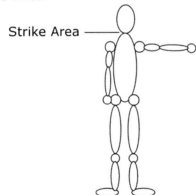

Strike Area

Alive Hand

The Alive Hand remains in the default position. It can be used to strike once the cane is wrapped around an opponent's neck (as in Fig. 103) or to pull down on the shaft when executing the chokehold.

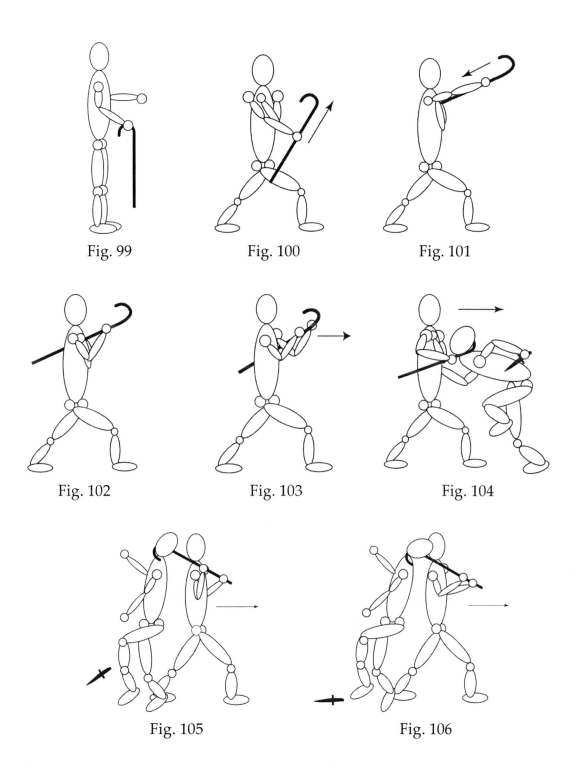

Fig. 99

Fig. 100

Fig. 101

Fig. 102

Fig. 103

Fig. 104

Fig. 105

Fig. 106

Weak-Side High-Level Strike

Technique
From the neutral stance (see Fig. 107 opposite), move into a weak stance and bring the cane around your strong side (the tip points toward your strong side) in a circular motion (Fig. 108).

Once your thumb is parallel with your forearm (Fig. 109), bring the arm and shoulder toward your strong side (Fig. 110). Use your hips and lateral muscles to generate power.

Remember to carry the strike completely through the motion. Your wrist will be in an awkward position (palm facing the strong side and the blade of your hand parallel with your shoulder), so you may want to practice this strike on a heavy bag and thus develop power.

Strike Areas

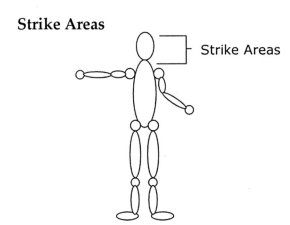

Strike Areas

Alive Hand
The Alive Hand should remain in its default position.

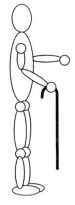

Fig. 107

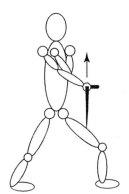

Fig. 108

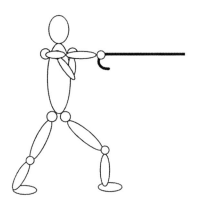

Fig. 109

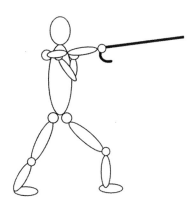

Fig. 110

Strong-Side High-Level Strike

Technique

From the neutral stance (see Fig. 111 opposite), assume a strong stance and bring the cane around your weak side in a circular motion—the tip points toward your weak side (Fig. 112).

Once your thumb parallels your forearm, bring the arm and shoulder toward your weak side (Fig. 113).

Strike the target with the end of the shaft. Remember to carry the strike all the way through—do not stop until the cane is literally wrapped around the weak side of your body (Fig. 114). Use you hips and lateral muscles to generate power.

Strike Areas

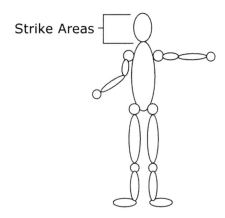

Alive Hand

The Alive Hand can help protect you from any blows that may come in while your are executing the strike.

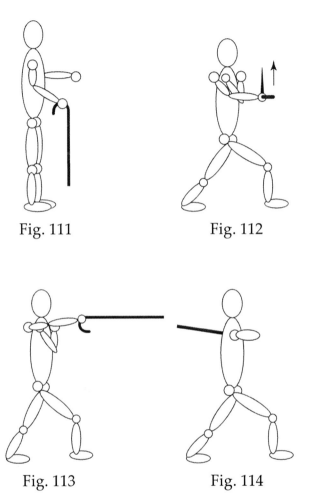

Fig. 111

Fig. 112

Fig. 113

Fig. 114

Weak-Side Corkscrew Thrust

Technique

From the neutral stance (see Fig. 115 opposite), assume a strong stance and hold the cane so that its tip points upward (Fig. 116). Twist the cane so that the shaft points toward your weak side and is perpendicular to your body (Fig. 117).

As you lean forward, placing more and more weight on the strong foot, twist the cane so that the shaft travels across your weak side until the tip points away from you (Fig. 118). From here twist the cane once again, this time so that the shaft's tip points upward (Fig. 119).

With the majority of your weight on your strong foot, twist the cane one final time so that the tip is driven into the opponent's upper body or head (Fig. 120). Drive the cane's tip into the target.

Remember to use your hips and legs to generate additional power. Make sure to maintain your balance; do not lean too far out, for such a move may make you vulnerable to attack.

Strike Areas

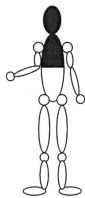

Alive Hand

The Alive hand remains in its default position. Use it to deflect any strikes that may come in while executing this strike.

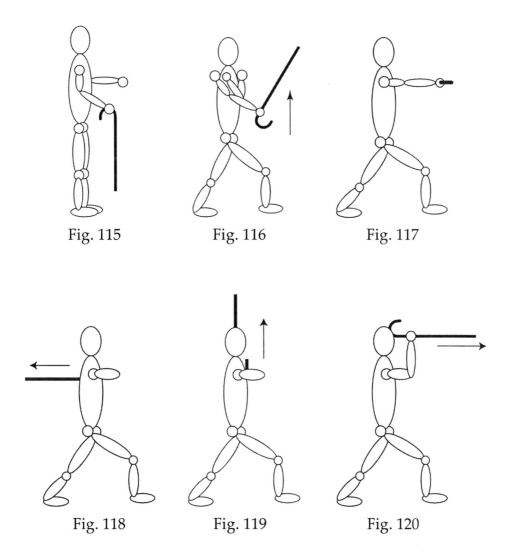

Fig. 115   Fig. 116   Fig. 117

Fig. 118   Fig. 119   Fig. 120

Strong-Side Axe Strike

Technique

From the neutral stance (see Fig. 121 opposite), assume a weak stance and bring your arm slightly back (Fig. 122). Bring the cane around your body as though you were swinging an axe (Fig. 123). Make sure the tip points upward.

Drive the cane downward (Fig. 124). Aim for the head or collarbone. Use your shoulders and arms to generate power.

Strike Areas

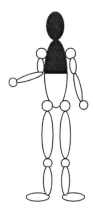

Alive Hand

The Alive Hand remains in its default position. It can be used to block any incoming attacks during the execution of this strike.

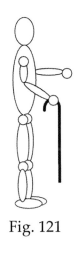

Fig. 121

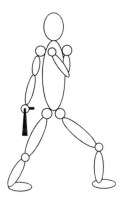

Fig. 122

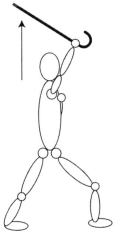

Fig. 123

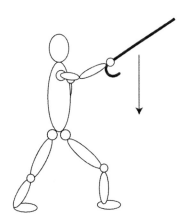

Fig. 124

The Flow

To practice the thirteen aforementioned strikes, the Goju-Shorei Weapons Branch has developed a set that flows from one strike to another. To achieve a yellow belt in this system, you must demonstrate the set four times as follows:

- right handed, static;
- left handed, static;
- right handed, moving; and
- left handed, moving.

By practicing with both hands, not only will you develop the beginnings of ambidexterity, but you also will learn a full complement of basic strikes. For example, you will learn the mirror images of the groin thrust and the axe strike.

As part of the flow, it is necessary to "pull" your strikes. The idea is to quickly switch from one strike to another. Thus, instead of carrying a Strong-Side Low-Level Strike all the way through, stop at the midpoint then execute a Weak-Side Low-Level Strike.

To enhance your power and fighting ability, practice these strikes on a heavy bag. Move from one strike to the other. Begin to manipulate your body by changing positions (for example, strike from a crouch). Such practice will enable you to move from strike to strike with ease.

Executing the Strike Set

The following three pages illustrate the complete strike set (sequence numbers 1-43).

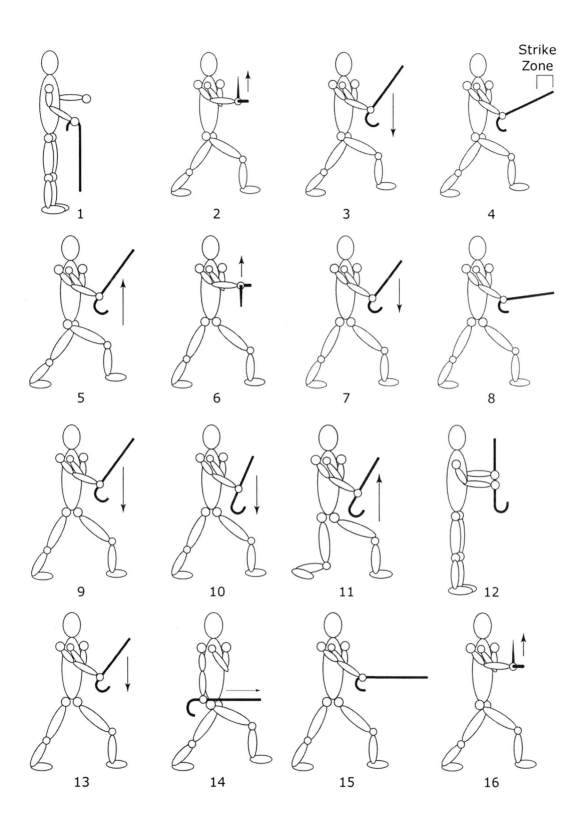

Strike
Zone

1   2   3   4

5   6   7   8

9   10   11   12

13   14   15   16

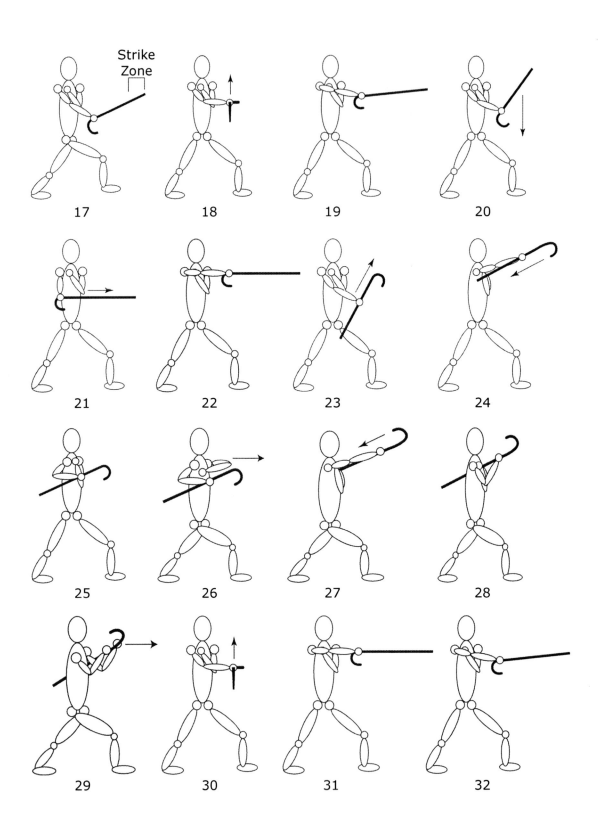

Strike
Zone

17

18

19

20

21

22

23

24

25

26

27

28

29

30

31

32

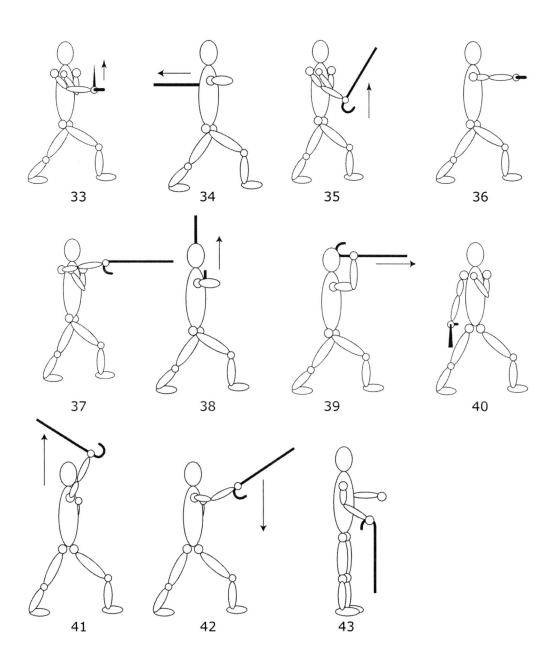

33

34

35

36

37

38

39

40

41

42

43

Supplemental Strikes

This section covers techniques that are not part of the strike set. There are literally hundreds upon hundreds of strikes designed for the cane. As you advance in your study of this weapon, you will begin to create your own strike sets and drills.

Foot Smash

Technique
From the neutral stance (see Fig. 125 opposite), move into a strong stance and keep the cane's tip pointed down. Bring the cane quickly forward (Fig. 126) and upward (Fig. 127).

With as much force as possible, drive the cane's tip into an opponent's foot, preferably in the "meaty" area before the toes (Fig. 128). Use your shoulders and legs to generate power. If necessary, crouch slightly to drive the cane deeper into the opponent's foot.

Strike Areas

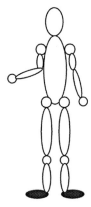

Strike Areas (in black)

Alive Hand
The Alive Hand can be used to deflect any strikes coming in from an opponent. It also can be used to generate additional power by helping drive the cane downward.

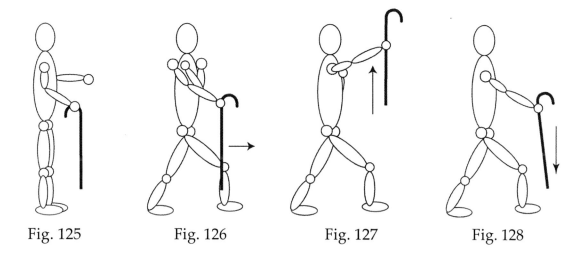

Fig. 125   Fig. 126   Fig. 127   Fig. 128

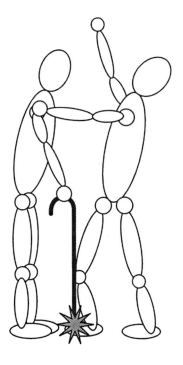

A foot smash is an ideal response against anyone attempting to grab or bear hug you. This technique works well in responding to either front or rear attacks.

Ankle Takedown

Technique

From the neutral stance (see Fig. 129 opposite), move into a strong stance and bring the cane down so that the horn faces away from you (Fig. 130). As you close distance, thrust the cane's shaft forward, wrapping the crook around the opponent's ankle (Fig. 131).

With as much force as you can muster, pull the cane toward you, thus knocking the opponent of his or her feet (Fig. 132). Use your shoulders and legs to generate the necessary power.

Strike Areas

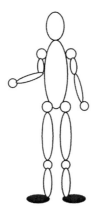

Strike Areas (in black)

Alive Hand

As you move into a strong stance, throw an elbow or palm-heel strike from your weak side (Fig. 133). With your opponent busy defending against such a strike, you can use the cane's crook to execute an ankle takedown.

The Alive Hand can also be used to generate additional power in pulling back the cane.

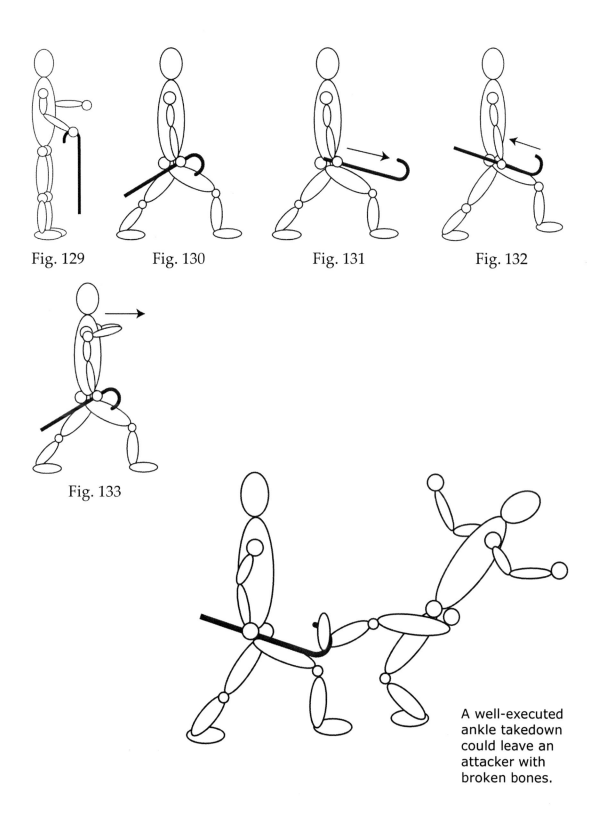

Fig. 129

Fig. 130

Fig. 131

Fig. 132

Fig. 133

A well-executed
ankle takedown
could leave an
attacker with
broken bones.

Ankle/Knee Strike with Horn

Technique

From the neutral stance (see Fig. 134 opposite), move into a strong stance. Raise the cane upward and at the same time bring the weapon hand down to the cane's tip (Fig. 135). With all the force you can muster, use your wrist to swing down the cane toward an opponent's ankle or knee, striking the target with the cane's horn (Fig. 136). Use your shoulders and hips like a golfer to generate power.

Strike Areas

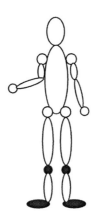

Strike Areas (in black)

Alive Hand

The Alive Hand remains in its default position. It can be used to deflect any incoming blows if necessary.

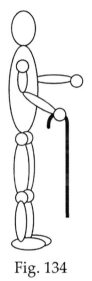

Fig. 134

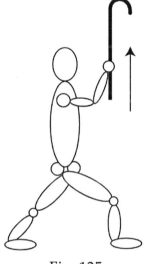

Fig. 135

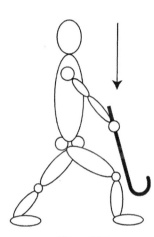

Fig. 136

Rib Thrust

Technique

From the neutral stance (see Fig. 137 opposite, front view), raise the cane to chest level and clasp it with both hands so that the palms face downward. The crook and horn should point toward the Alive Hand's thumb (Fig. 138).

As quickly as possible, dig the horn into the opponent's rib cage, if possible between two ribs. Pull the cane's shaft with as much force as possible while digging the cane's horn into the rib cage. Use both hands if necessary. Figure 139 shows the alignment of the cane with the opponent's rib cage.

Strike Areas

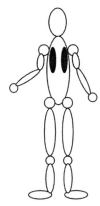

Strike Areas (in black)

Alive Hand

The Alive Hand can be used to generate additional power when pulling the cane against the rib cage.

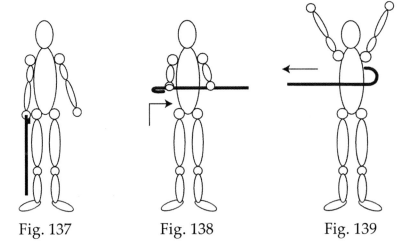

Fig. 137   Fig. 138   Fig. 139

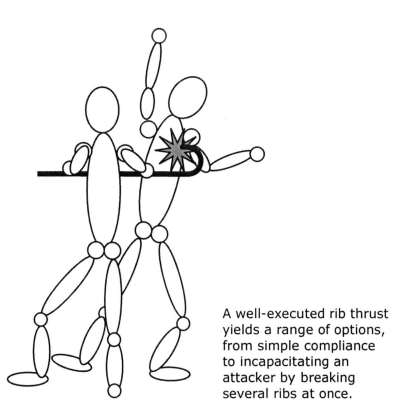

A well-executed rib thrust yields a range of options, from simple compliance to incapacitating an attacker by breaking several ribs at once.

Collarbone Drop

Technique

From the neutral stance (see Fig 140 opposite), assume a weak stance and have the cane's horn point away from your body (crook out), as shown in Fig. 141. Raise the cane up so that the horn is above an opponent's shoulder (Fig. 142).

With all the force you can generate, quickly bring down the cane so that the horn hooks the opponent's collarbone or shoulder (preferably in the rotator cuff), as shown in Fig. 143. If necessary, drop to your knees, all the time digging the horn into the opponent's soft muscle areas. It does not matter which side of the body you elect to target.

Strike Areas

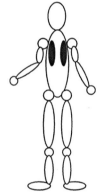

Strike Areas (in black)

Alive Hand
The Alive Hand can be used to generate additional power when pulling down the cane.

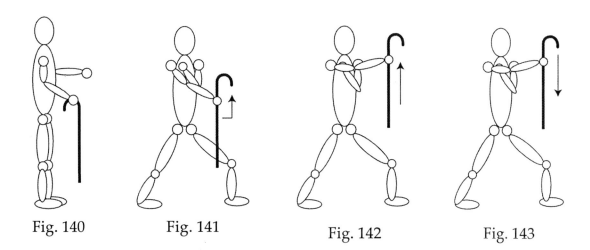

Fig. 140   Fig. 141   Fig. 142   Fig. 143

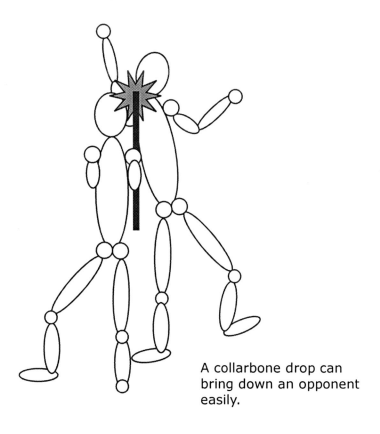

A collarbone drop can bring down an opponent easily.

Fan Strike

Technique

From the neutral stance (see Fig. 144 opposite), assume a strong stance and bring the cane up so that it is perpendicular to your forearm, with the tip pointed behind you (Fig. 145, reverse angle).

Using your wrist as a fulcrum, launch the cane's tip forward (Fig. 146) until it is once again perpendicular to your forearm (Fig. 147), at which point the wrist will stop the cane's momentum. This technique requires much practice (and strong wrists) before it becomes effective.

Once you have "flicked" the cane's tip forward, you can quickly reverse the steps and thus prepare for more fan strikes or other follow-up techniques.

The preferred targets for this strike are the collarbones and shoulders. However, an extended knee (i.e., a kicking knee) or the head also can be considered targets.

Strike Areas

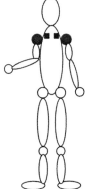

Strike Areas (in black)

Alive Hand

The Alive Hand remains in its default position during the execution of this strike.

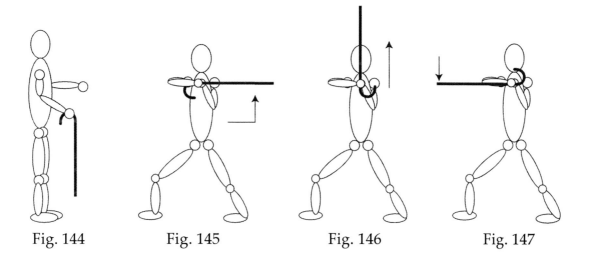

Fig. 144   Fig. 145   Fig. 146   Fig. 147

Horn Strike to Face

Technique

From the neutral stance (see Fig. 148 opposite, front view), assume a strong stance and bring the cane up (bring your forearms up into your face) so that it is perpendicular to the neck area (Fig. 149).

As quickly as possible, dig the horn into an opponent's face, preferably along the nose or cheekbone (Fig. 150). Pull the cane's shaft with as much force as possible while digging the cane's horn into the face.

Strike Areas

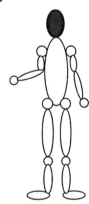

Strike Areas (in black)

Alive Hand

The Alive Hand remains in its default position during the execution of this strike.

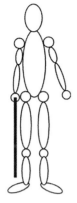

Fig. 148

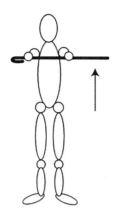

Fig. 149

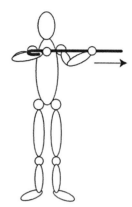

Fig. 150

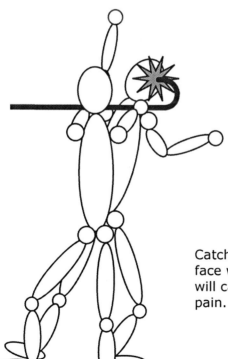

Catching any part of the face with the cane's horn will cause tremendous pain.

Horn Jab to Hand

Technique

From the neutral stance (see Fig. 151 opposite), bring the cane up to chest level and turn the horn so that it faces either your thumb or index finger (Fig. 152). With as much power as possible, bring the cane down an opponent's hand (the one you have access to; it does not matter which one), driving the horn into the fleshy area between the fingers and wrist (Fig. 153).

This technique can be used when an opponent grabs you by the chest or shoulders. Even if your shoulders are immobilized, you still can bring the cane up and place the horn on the opponent's hand. It does not take much pressure to cause extreme discomfort in this area.

Strike Areas

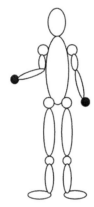

Strike Areas (in black)

Alive Hand

The Alive Hand can be used to generate additional power when driving the cane downward or it can be used to execute a palm-heel strike or throw an elbow at the opponent's head.

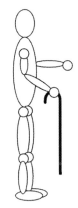

Fig. 151

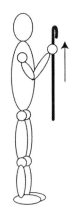

Fig. 152

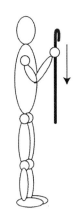

Fig. 153

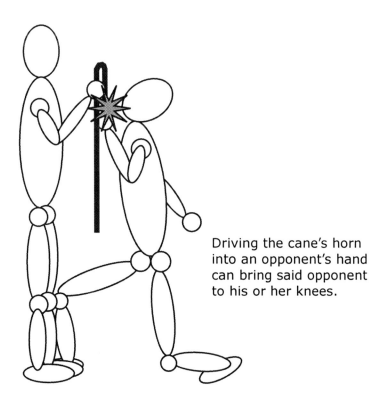

Driving the cane's horn into an opponent's hand can bring said opponent to his or her knees.

Shaft Strike to Neck

Technique

This is simply a "clothesline" technique, but instead of using your arm you use the cane's shaft, which is much less forgiving.

From the neutral stance (Fig. 154), move into a strong stance and bring the cane up to chest level, with the shaft parallel to your shoulders but with the weak-side tip slightly elevated (Fig. 155).

As the opponent closes distance, slightly step to the strong side, bringing the cane's shaft into the opponent's neck. Slightly twist the cane so that the strong end is elevated (Fig. 156).

Use your legs and hips to drive the cane into the neck. Use both hands to generate additional power. To take the opponent to the ground, take a step forward as you execute this strike.

Strike Area

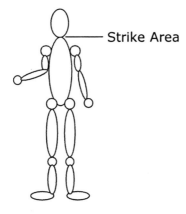

Strike Area

Alive Hand

The Alive Hand can be used to generate additional power when driving the cane into the opponent's neck.

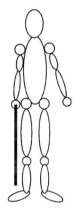

Fig. 154

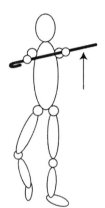

Fig. 155

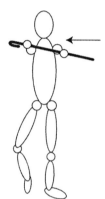

Fig. 156

Bear Hug Release

Technique

This technique can be used when an attacker grabs you by the throat or executes any type of "bear hug" maneuver (even if an opponent grabs you by the shoulders).

As the opponent grabs you, maneuver the cane so that it is perpendicular to your body, preferably with the crook pointed toward the opponent (see Fig. 157 opposite). Bring the cane forward so that the crook is beyond the opponent's back (Fig. 158).

With as much power as possible, drive the cane's horn into the opponent's lower back (Fig. 159). Use your shoulders and hips to generate additional power. Figure 160 shows a variation of this technique in which the cane's tip is used. Either end of the cane is effective.

Strike Area

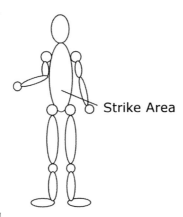

Strike Area

Alive Hand

You could use the Alive Hand to:

- distract (e.g., slap your opponent),
- incapacitate (e.g., gouge the eyes, tear at the nose, ears, or mouth), or
- execute a follow-up technique once you are released (palm-heel strike, elbow, or other form of attack).

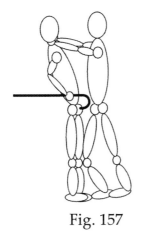

Fig. 157

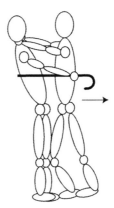

Fig. 158

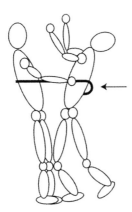

Fig. 159

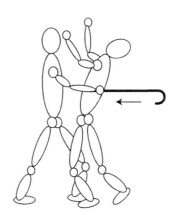

Fig. 160

Shoulder Grab Release

Technique
This technique is simply a variation of the bear hug release. It is also effective when escaping from an attacker who hopes to immobilize your shoulders.

As an opponent grabs you by the shoulders, bring the cane up so that the tip and horn face away from you (see Fig. 161 opposite). With as much force as possible, drive the cane upward and between the opponent's arms, using the horn to strike his or her chin (Fig. 162).

If the opponent somehow manages to hold on, quickly turn the cane so that it stretches across the opponent's arms. Drive the cane down, slamming the shaft onto the opponent's biceps or wrists (Fig. 163). Use enough force so that you break the opponent's grip completely (Fig. 164).

After breaking free, you may opt to create distance or follow-up with a take-down (e.g., wrap the cane around the neck and pull opponent to the ground).

Strike Areas

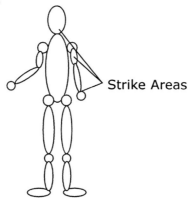

Strike Areas

Alive Hand
The Alive Hand can be used to generate additional power when driving the cane into the opponent's chin and when slamming down the cane onto the opponent's arms.

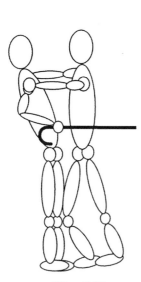

Fig. 161

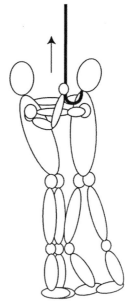

Fig. 162

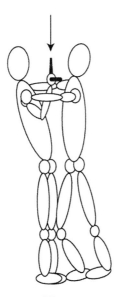

Fig. 163

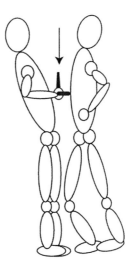

Fig. 164

Leashing the Bulldog

Technique

Inexperienced fighters and some overanxious grapplers may attempt to rush you, thus taking you to the ground (a grappler's environment). This technique is designed to thwart such fighters.

As an opponent charges you (see Fig. 165 opposite), you can elect to side-step (i.e., get out of the line of attack) or if he or she is too close, bring the cane toward your weak side (Fig. 166) and concurrently raise a knee aimed at his or her gut (Fig. 167). Drive the knee into the opponent's gut with as much power as possible.

As soon as possible, retract the knee (and strike again and again if necessary) and step forward, bringing the crook of the cane toward the opponent's neck. Wrap the crook around the opponent's neck (Fig. 168) and pull the shaft away from your chest (Fig. 169). Take the opponent to the ground and follow up as necessary.

Strike Areas

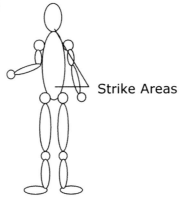

Strike Areas

Alive Hand

The Alive Hand can deliver an additional strike (e.g., a palm-heel strike or an elbow strike) along with the knee strike. Alternatively, the Alive-Hand can, if necessary, provide additional force in pulling the cane.

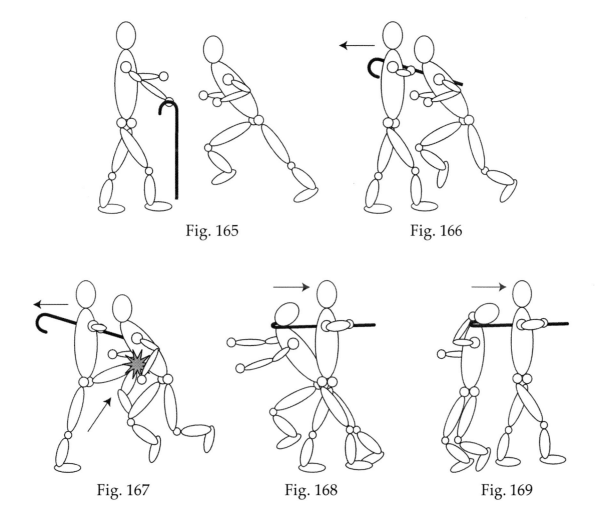

Fig. 165

Fig. 166

Fig. 167

Fig. 168

Fig. 169

Shovel Strike

Technique
This style of thrust is designed to take down an opponent with one solid strike. From the neutral stance (see Fig. 170 opposite), assume a strong stance, draw the cane back with the weapon hand, and grasp the shaft with the Alive Hand (Fig. 171). Note how the cane's position is "cocked" liked a bolt on a crossbow.

With all the power you can generate, drive the cane forward at an angle (Fig. 172). Targets include the sternum, under the chin, or even the nose or an eye. The shaft in this case can be considered a "shovel's blade" and the thrust is designed to literally "cut into" an opponent. Figure 173 shows the thrust under an opponent's chin.

Figures 174-176 show this strike in response to a rear assault.

Strike Area

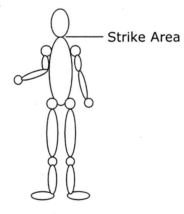

Alive Hand
The Alive Hand is used to drive the cane into an opponent's target area.

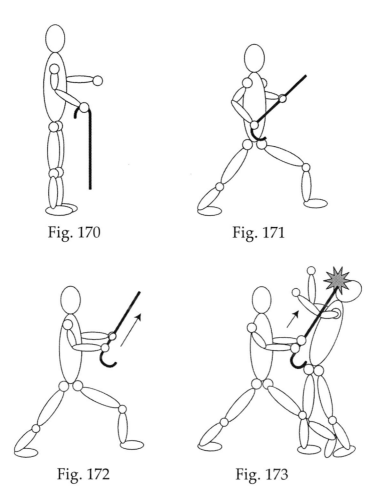

Fig. 170

Fig. 171

Fig. 172

Fig. 173

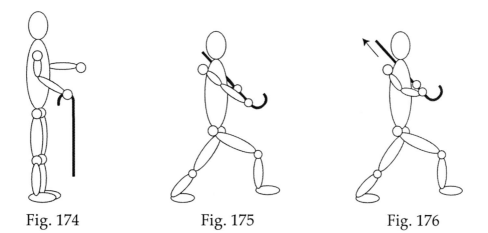

Fig. 174

Fig. 175

Fig. 176

Helicopter Blades

Technique

This is a combination strike with a specific target area: the head. The strike begins like Power Strike Two: Sweep Up. From the cocked position (see Fig. 177 opposite), bring the cane upward in a diagonal fashion (Fig. 178).

Use your wrist to twist the cane (clockwise if you are right-hand dominant) around so that the tip points to your weak side (figs. 179-180). Flicking the cane, bring it forward, using the tip to strike at the head (Fig. 181). If possible, target the temple.

Quickly reverse the cane's momentum, bring the cane around to your strong side (counterclockwise if you are right-hand dominant, as shown in figs. 182-183).

From this position, flick the cane (Fig. 184) once again, targeting the head and the other temple.

After these two strikes, you can opt to repeat the technique (hence the helicopter label) or swing the cane around your head and following up with a Sweep Down Power Strike.

Strike Areas

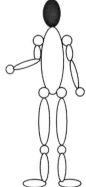

Strike Areas (in black)

Alive Hand

The Alive Hand remains in its default position during the execution of this strike.

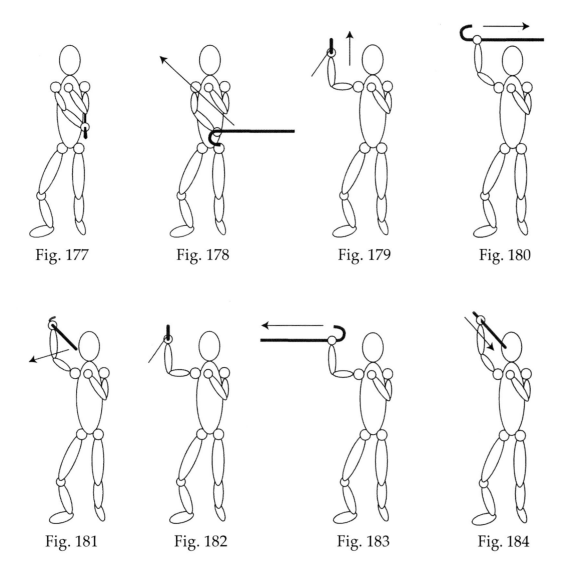

Fig. 177   Fig. 178   Fig. 179   Fig. 180

Fig. 181   Fig. 182   Fig. 183   Fig. 184

Part Three
Blocks

Block Set and Flow

This section presents 16 basic blocks. This set is part of the training necessary to obtain a yellow belt in the Goju-Shorei Weapons Branch. Practice these techniques with your left and right arm so that both can gain equal proficiency.

Weak-Side Broom Block

Technique

So-called because of their sweeping-like motion, broom blocks are designed to deflect low-level attacks, such as kicks or weapon strikes to the toes, ankles, shins, and knees.

From the neutral stance (see Fig. 185 opposite), bring the cane up, grasping it with both hands, and at the same time assume a strong-side stance (Fig. 186). As the opponent executes an attack to your weak side, "sweep" the cane along your lower body, making sure that the shaft is not too close to your body (Fig. 187). A strong strike can knock the cane into your body.

Sweep the cane as far as you need, twisting your body if necessary (Fig. 188). Be prepared to follow-up immediately with a barrage of strikes after deflecting an attack, particularly if your opponent attempts a kick. Recovering from a kick takes time, and in that time you can execute several power strikes and take down the opponent.

Defensive Areas

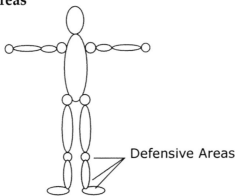

Defensive Areas

Alive Hand

Use the Alive Hand to support the cane's shaft while executing this technique. Both hands will enable you to deflect stronger blows.

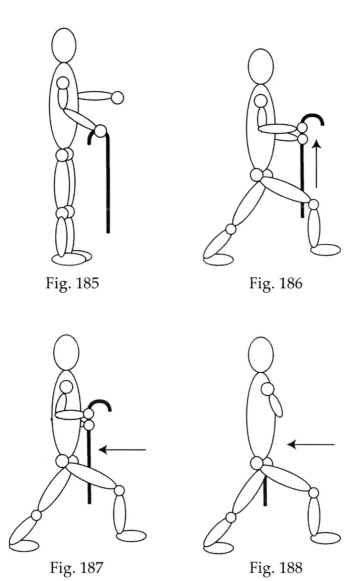

Fig. 185

Fig. 186

Fig. 187

Fig. 188

Strong-Side Broom Block

Technique
This is the mirror image of the Weak-Side Broom Block.

From the neutral stance (see Fig. 189 opposite), bring the cane up, grasping it with both hands, and at the same time assume a weak-side stance (Fig. 190). As the opponent executes an attack to your strong side, sweep the cane along your lower body, making sure that the shaft is not too close to your body (Fig. 191). A strong strike can knock the cane into your body.

Sweep the cane as far as you need, twisting your body if necessary (Fig. 192). Be prepared to follow-up immediately with a barrage of strikes after deflecting an attack, particularly if your opponent attempts a kick.

Defensive Areas

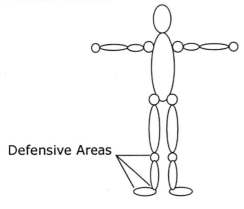

Defensive Areas

Alive Hand
Use the Alive Hand to support the cane's shaft during this technique. Using both hands will enable you to deflect stronger blows.

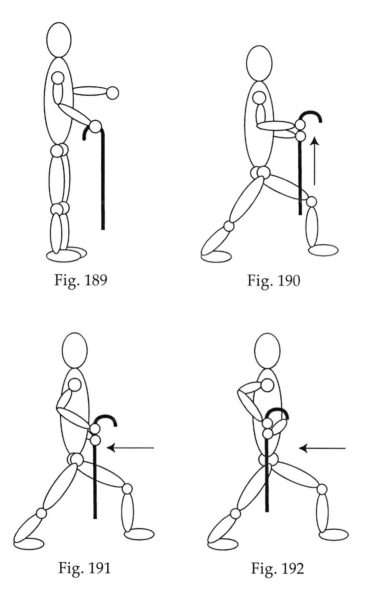

Fig. 189

Fig. 190

Fig. 191

Fig. 192

Strong-Side Low Block

Technique

This block is designed to block low-angle attacks, such as a strike to the groin. It is very effective against large weapons, such as staffs, pool cues, or iron pipes.

From the neutral stance (see Fig. 193 opposite), move into a strong-side stance and begin to bring the cane around your body in a circular motion (Fig. 194). Use your wrist and forearm to generate speed. Bring the cane down to your torso and begin to move the Alive Hand toward the cane's shaft (Fig. 195).

Grasp the cane with both hands (Fig. 196) and drive the cane into the attacking appendage or weapon (Fig. 197). Be prepared to follow-up with an offensive maneuver of your own. Do not stay in this position for long because it does present some vulnerabilities.

Defensive Area

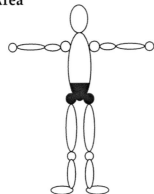

Alive Hand

The Alive Hand is used to support the cane's shaft when executing the low strike.

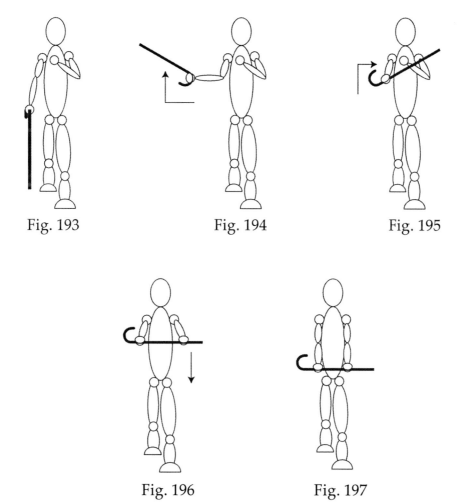

Fig. 193

Fig. 194

Fig. 195

Fig. 196

Fig. 197

Weak-Side Mid-Level Block

Technique

From the neutral stance (see Fig. 198 opposite), assume a weak stance and twist the cane upward (Fig. 199) until the its tip points up (Fig. 200). Drop your weight onto the back leg and twist your body slightly toward the weak side, bringing the cane with you (see the arrow in Fig. 200).

While doing this, take the Alive Hand off the heart and bring it back, opening the hand so that the palm faces outward and the back of the thumb rests against your chest. Let the shaft rest on the palm of the hand and tighten the grip on the weapon hand (Fig. 201).

Do not attempt to grab the cane with the Alive Hand. Doing so would make your hand a target. Brace the shaft as best you can using the palm of your hand, particularly if a strike comes from a heavy weapon, such as a staff or pool cue.

Defensive Area

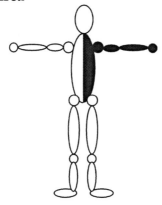

Alive Hand

The Alive Hand is opened and the palm used to brace the shaft.

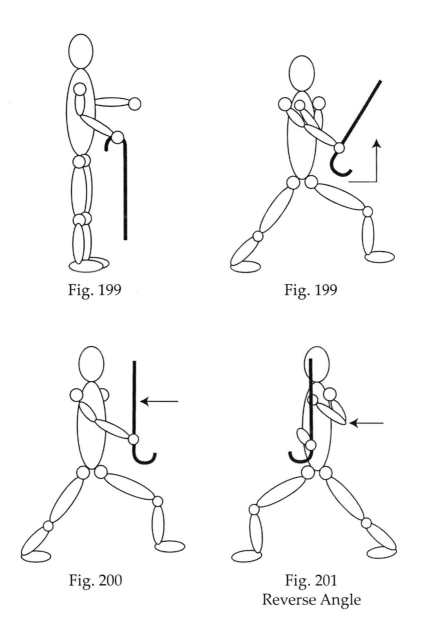

Fig. 199

Fig. 199

Fig. 200

Fig. 201
Reverse Angle

Strong-Side Mid-Level Block

Technique

This is the mirror image of the Weak-Side Mid-Level Block; see Figs 202-205 opposite. In this block, however, you must bring the Alive Hand across the body to support the shaft. As a result, the fingers of your Alive Hand may be perpendicular to the shaft, with the elbow consequently sticking out.

If this happens, quickly tuck in your elbow so that the fingers run parallel with the shaft. If you allow your elbow to stick out then it may be hit, resulting in severe pain and possibly a disabled arm.

Defensive Area

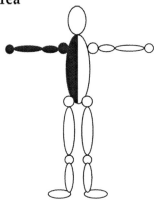

Alive Hand

The Alive Hand is opened and the palm used to brace the shaft. Figure 206 shows this defense at work.

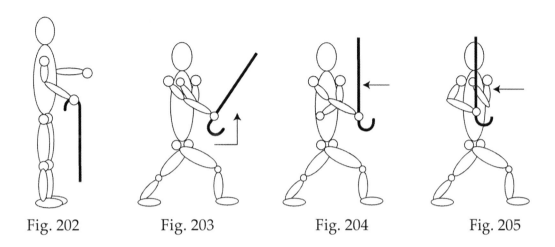

Fig. 202   Fig. 203   Fig. 204   Fig. 205

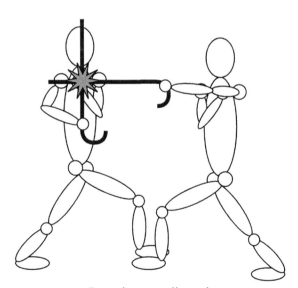

Guard your elbow by
keeping it tucked in as
you support the cane
with your Alive Hand.

Weak-Side Roof Block

Technique

This overhead block is designed to deflect strikes to the weak side of the head, neck, and shoulder.

From the neutral stance (see Fig. 206 opposite), shift into a strong stance and concurrently bring the cane up at an angle (Fig. 207). As you bring the cane over your head at an angle that resembles one-half of a pitched roof, bring the Alive Hand, palm open, upward as well, to reinforce the shaft (Fig. 208).

As the strike comes, push both arms out at an angle, deflecting the blow (Fig. 209). Catch the blow in the middle of the shaft; work hard to avoid letting your hands become a target, making sure the Alive Hand remains open and free to move about. From this position you may opt to follow up with a power strike or with a thrust.

The roof block serves as the basis for a later block known as the "Opening of the Umbrella". This block is extremely effective and will be discussed in detail in *Part Four: Fighting.*

Defensive Area

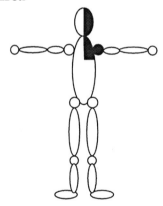

Alive Hand

Use the Alive Hand to brace the roof block. Make sure to keep your hand open and to shift the shaft so that neither hand becomes a target.

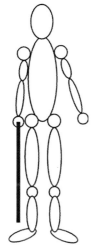

Fig. 206

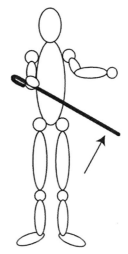

Fig. 207

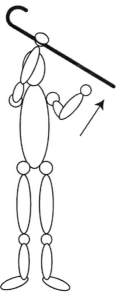

Fig. 208

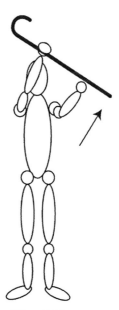

Fig. 209

Strong-Side Roof Block

Technique

This is the mirror image of the Weak-Side Roof Block, only this time the block is used to protect the body's strong side; see Figs 210-212 opposite.

A particularly effective follow-up strike would be a jab with the cane's horn to the opponent's face. To add power to the strike, both hands would grasp the cane as the horn is drawn across the face or ear.

Defensive Area

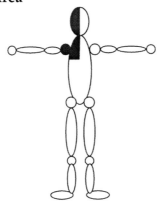

Alive Hand

Use the Alive Hand to brace the roof block. Make sure to keep your hand open and to shift the shaft so that neither hand becomes a target.

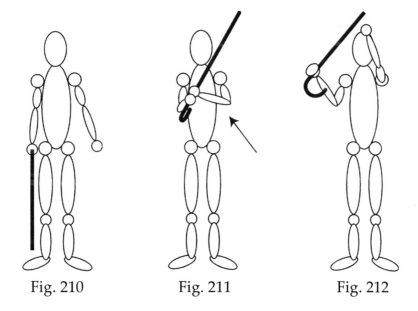

Fig. 210   Fig. 211   Fig. 212

Overhead Roof Block

Technique

From the neutral stance (see Fig. 213 opposite), assume a weak stance and bring the cane around so that the shaft is perpendicular to your body (Fig. 214). Raise the cane above and away from your head (Fig. 215). Figure 216 presents the block as a side view so that you can determine proper position.

As the opponent's weapon or body strike comes in, use both hands to push off the strike, thus minimizing its impact.

Defensive Area

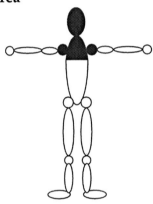

Alive Hand

Use the Alive Hand to brace the shaft against heavy blows, particularly power shots from weapons. Keep the Alive Hand's palm open; do not grasp the shaft.

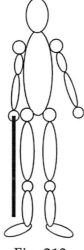

Fig. 213

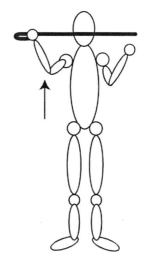

Fig. 214

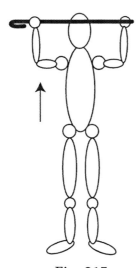

Fig. 215

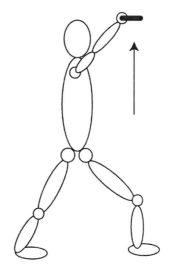

Fig. 216

Weak-Side Down Parry Block

Technique
This striking block is designed to defend against a strike to the weak-side leg, including the knee and ankle. Practice this strike many times to develop timing and power to deflect a serious blow.

From the neutral stance (see Fig. 217 opposite), assume a strong stance, in the process removing the weak leg from a strike (Fig. 218). As you assume the stance, begin to bring the cane around you in a circle in front of you. Bring the cane around (Fig. 219) so that it eventually comes around your strong side (Fig. 220), striking the opponent's strike next to the strong leg (Fig. 221).

Notice the placement of your wrist at the completion of this strike. Do not keep the wrist like this for long because it is vulnerable. Once the blow is deflected, follow up with a strike or create distance.

Defensive Area

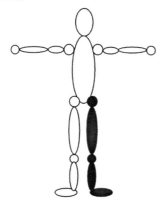

Alive Hand
The Alive Hand remains in its default position. If there is an opening, you can bring it forward to disrupt the opponent by tearing at his or her face.

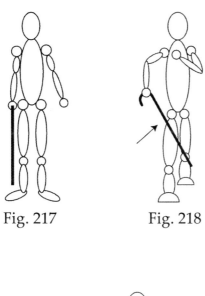

Fig. 217

Fig. 218

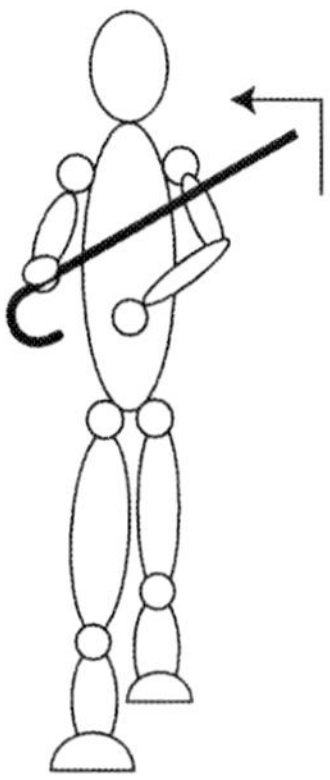

Fig. 219

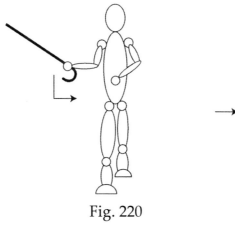

Fig. 220

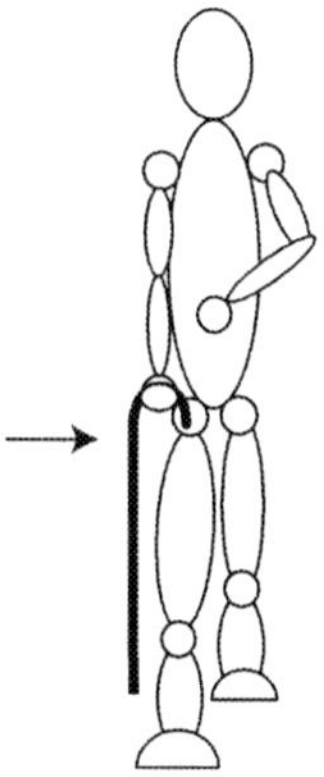

Fig. 221

Strong-Side Down Parry Block

Technique
This is the mirror image of the Weak-Side Down Parry Block, only this one is designed to defend the strong leg; see Figs 222-225 opposite.

Defensive Area

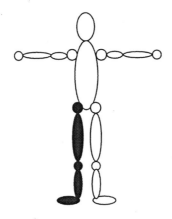

Alive Hand
The Alive Hand remains in its default position.

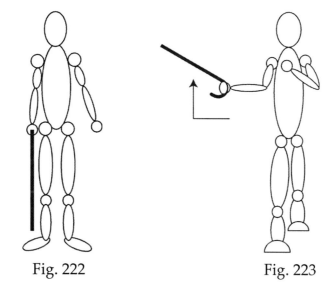

Fig. 222   Fig. 223

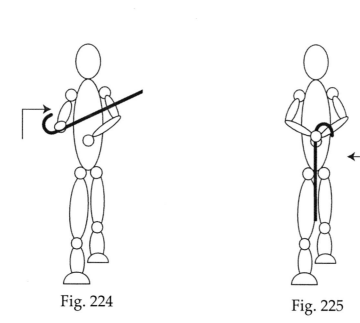

Fig. 224   Fig. 225

Strong-Side Step Offline Block

Technique

This blocking strike is designed to deflect thrusts to the trunk or head. It requires footwork and so must be practiced often to be executed easily during a fight.

From the neutral stance (see Fig. 226 opposite), begin to bring the cane up toward your weak side (Fig. 227) in a circular motion. As the cane begins to make its way toward your strong side (Fig. 228), side step by pivoting your feet so that they point to your strong side (Fig. 229).

Follow your feet by pivoting your body and then assume a strong stance from that position, as a result moving to one side and away from the thrust (Fig. 229).

From this position, bring the cane around your head (Fig. 230) and down toward your strong side (Fig. 231), striking the opponent's appendage (such as a kick) or weapon.

Defensive Area

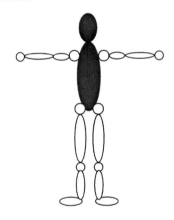

Alive Hand

The Alive Hand remains in its default position during this block.

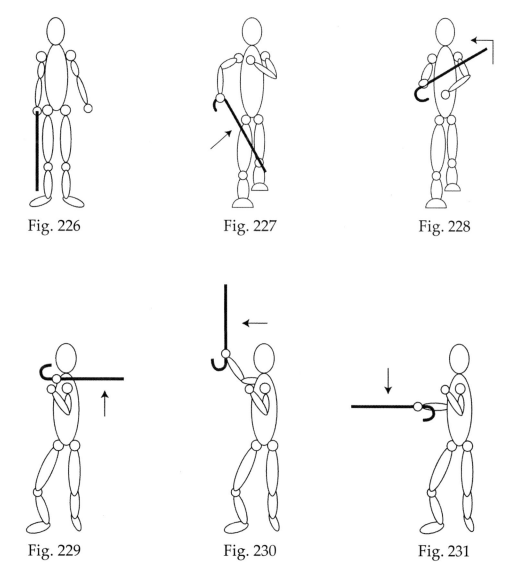

Fig. 226

Fig. 227

Fig. 228

Fig. 229

Fig. 230

Fig. 231

Weak-Side Step Offline Block

Technique

This is the mirror image of the Strong-Side Offline Block; see Figures 232-236 opposite. It requires footwork and so must be practiced often to be executed easily during a fight.

Defensive Area

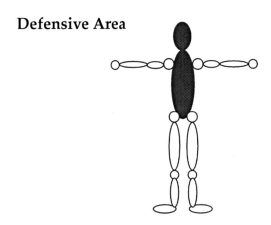

Alive Hand

The Alive Hand remains in its default position during this block.

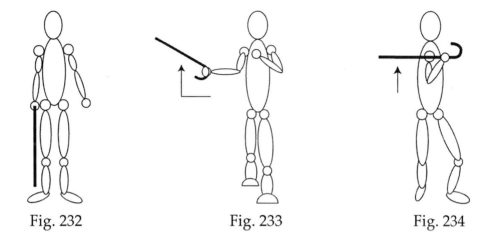

Fig. 232   Fig. 233   Fig. 234

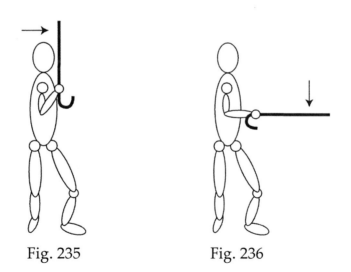

Fig. 235   Fig. 236

Weak-Side Fencer's Block

Technique

This block resembles the Weak-Side Broom Block, only this time the block is higher and the cane is held with the thumb and forefingers pointed down. This block is designed to protect against strikes to the weak side's head and torso.

From the neutral stance (see Fig. 237 opposite), assume a strong stance and bring the cane up and toward your weak side, twisting the forearm so that the palm faces away from you (Fig. 238). As you bring the cane higher, twist your body toward the weak side, bringing the cane with you (Fig. 239).

At the end of the block, your forearm should be across your face, along the nose, and your body should be twisted so that you present a minimal target to your opponent (Fig. 240, reverse angle).

Figure 241 shows how this block can be used to ward off an attack to the head.

Defensive Area

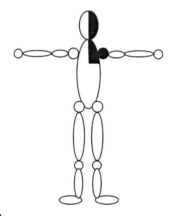

Alive Hand

The Alive Hand can be used to strengthen the block by supporting the cane's shaft.

In this case, you should grasp the shaft with the hand, being careful that it does not become a target. By grasping the cane with both hands, you can push off a heavy strike, particularly from a long or heavy weapon.

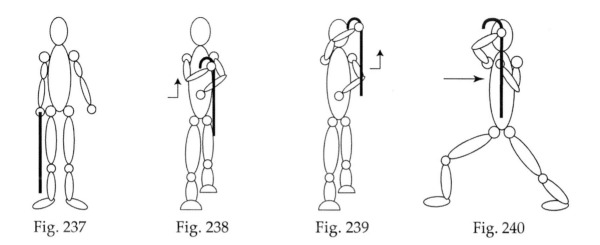

Fig. 237   Fig. 238   Fig. 239   Fig. 240

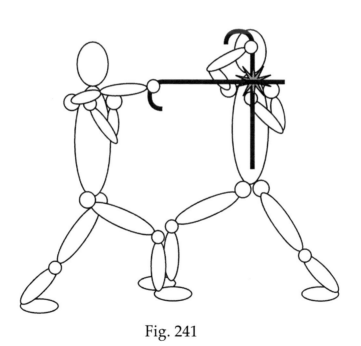

Fig. 241

Strong-Side Fencer's Block

Technique

This is the mirror image of the Weak-Side Fencer's Block; see Figures 242-245 opposite. For this block, make sure to keep your elbow back; do not let it point outward or it could become a target.

Defensive Area

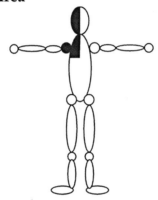

Alive Hand

The Alive Hand can be used to strengthen the block by supporting the cane's shaft. Because of the awkward placement of this block, it is not possible to push off a strike.

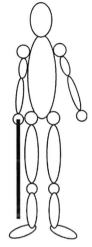

Fig. 242

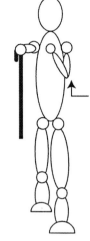

Fig. 243

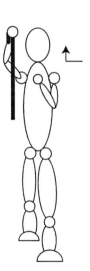

Fig. 244

Fig. 245

Closing the Umbrella

Technique

This block is an extension of the Weak-Side Roof Block, but it is designed as a striking block that wards off quick and powerful attacks. It is called an umbrella block because its execution mimics the closing of a parasol.

From the neutral stance (Fig. 246), assume a strong stance and at the same time bring both arms down, with the weapon hand pointing the shaft out so that it is perpendicular to the body, with the palm facing out (Fig. 247).

Quickly bring both arms up, twisting your weapon hand's wrist so that the palm faces you. As you do this, bring the cane up with the tip pointed down and at an angle (Fig. 248). Bring the cane up as though there were a weight on its tip.

Create the roof block (Fig. 249) and follow through by creating a straight roof block and then (Fig. 251) crossing both hands. Remember, this is a striking block, so draw the cane through the complete motion. In a fight, you will deflect an opponent's strike and draw the cane through so that you can strike back from a position of power.

From the ending motion (Fig. 251), you may elect to execute a Reverse Sweep Down or Reverse Horizontal Sweep. Either of these power strikes will clear the air quickly and effectively.

Defensive Area

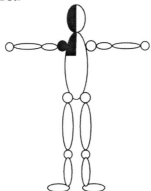

Alive Hand

The Alive Hand moves in conjunction with the weapon hand, subsequently crossing. This motion has no real significance other than to provide counterbalance for the block.

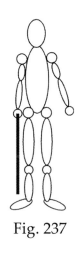

Fig. 237

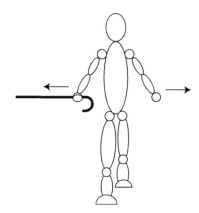

Fig. 238

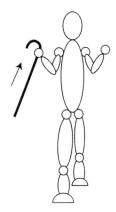

Fig. 239

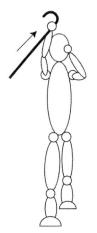

Fig. 237

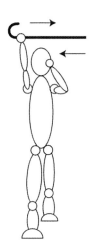

Fig. 238

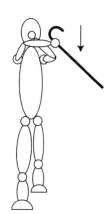

Fig. 239

Opening the Umbrella

Technique

This is the mirror image of Closing the Umbrella (see Figures 252 to 257 opposite). This blocking style is particularly useful when closing distance on an opponent. By stepping forward and deflecting an overhead blow (thus protecting the head and shoulder), it is then easy to take several quick steps into the opponent, executing follow-up strikes (such as multiple thrusts to the sternum or gut) and thus ending the fight.

Defensive Area

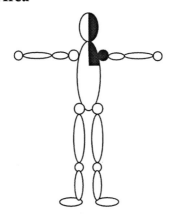

Alive Hand

The Alive Hand moves across the chest and pushes off the shaft as the weapon hand initiates the roof block. The hand then returns to its default position.

Executing the Block Set

Pages 120-123 illustrate the complete block set (sequence numbers 1-58).

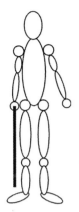

Fig. 252

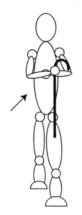

Fig. 253

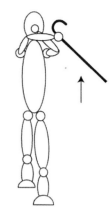

Fig. 254

Fig. 255

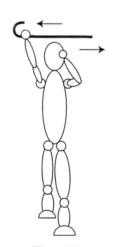

Fig. 256

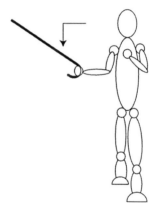

Fig. 257

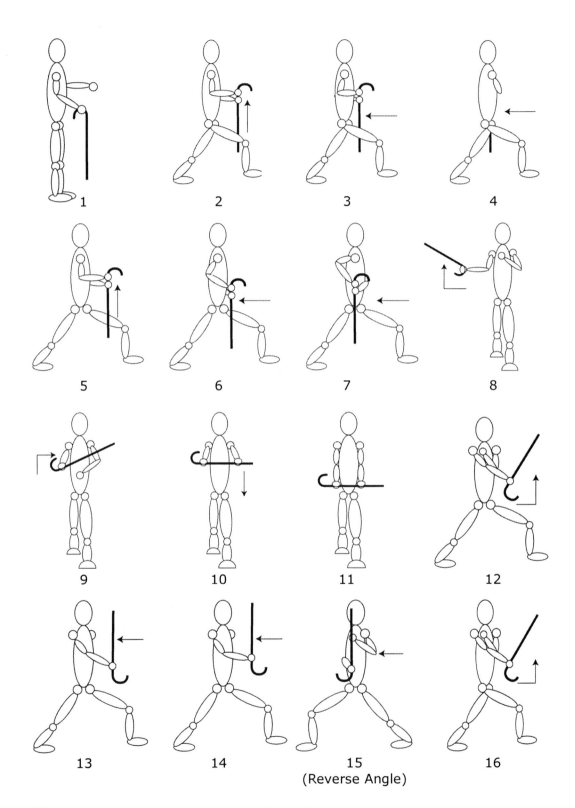

1

2

3

4

5

6

7

8

9

10

11

12

13

14

15
(Reverse Angle)

16

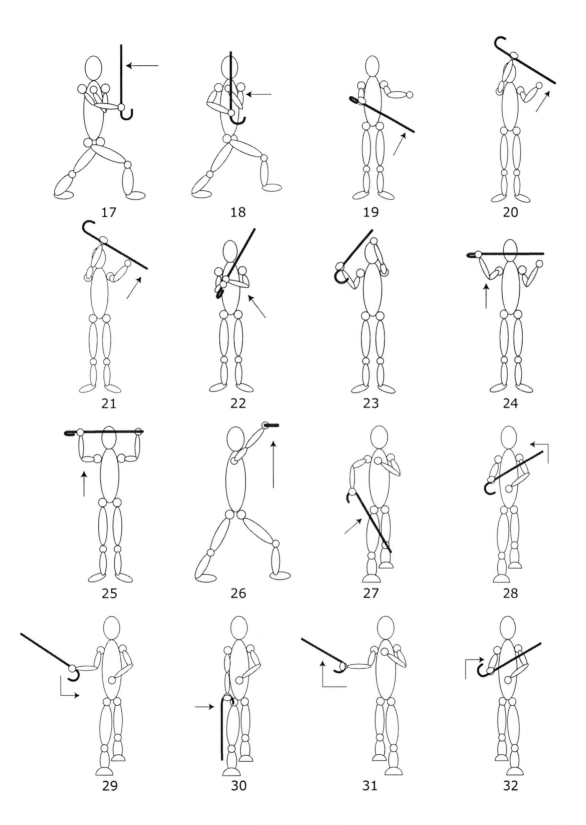

17   18   19   20

21   22   23   24

25   26   27   28

29   30   31   32

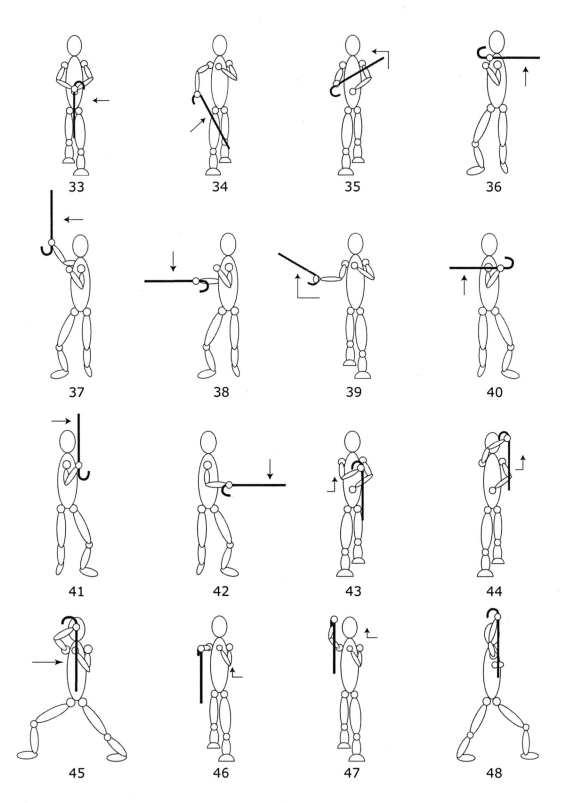

33

34

35

36

37

38

39

40

41

42

43

44

45

46

47

48

RAISING CANE

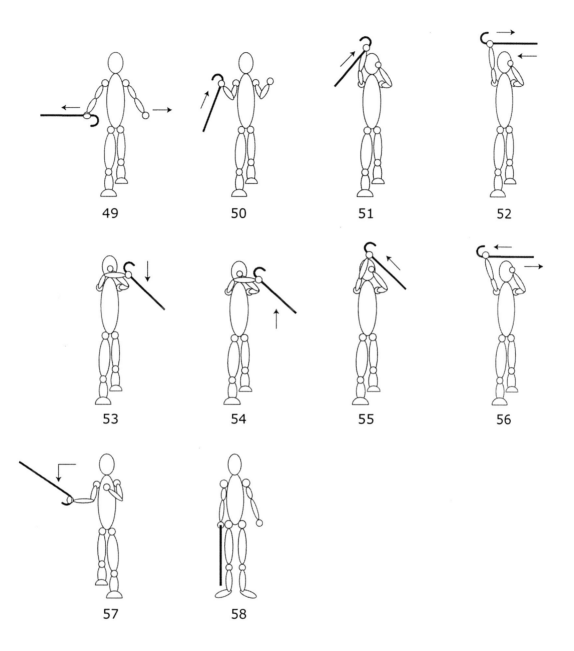

49

50

51

52

53

54

55

56

57

58

Part Four
Fighting

Introduction

Every day, predators walk the Earth in search of victims. In most cases, these predators are not skilled fighters. Their advantage is in selecting the weak. Once they have made a decision, they move in and take what they want, be it your valuables, body, or life.

In a street fight, there are no rules. Assailants will not wait for you to assume a special martial arts stance, nor will they punch or kick like a martial artist. A street fight is fast, dirty, brutal, and most importantly, unpredictable.

Building an Arsenal

The techniques shown in Parts Two and Three of this book are tools from which you can build a self-defense system tailored to meet your specific needs. Practice the flows constantly so you develop proficiency with every movement.

Most importantly, make sure to develop power with the two sets of Cinco Tiros. These are your most powerful strikes—they are designed to end a fight quickly and with finality.

The reason for so many strikes and blocks is that each has specific applications and target areas. By practicing these basics, you can prepare an arsenal of techniques that you can tap into during a conflict. For example, some blocks and strikes are ideal for the lower body, whereas others are designed to protect or attack the hand.

The following sections are designed to help you build a self-defense system tailored to your physical ability, dexterity skills, and personal needs.

Assessing the Threat

The first step in preparing for a street fight is assessing the threat. When carrying your cane, be ready to assume a fighting stance as soon as you recognize a threat. This will communicate two things to a potential assailant:

- you have recognized the threat and are prepared to address it.
- you have assumed a fighting position, which means that you have the fundamental skills to defend yourself.

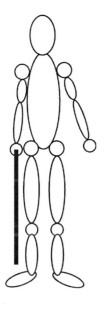

The neutral stance communicates nothing to an opponent. Because of the cane's acceptance in society, it is not perceived as a threat.

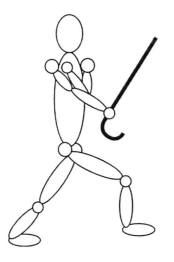

The strong stance prepares you for any threat. It also communicates to a potential assailant that you are prepared to mount a defense. From this simple stance, you can execute strikes (including the power strikes, which are your most devastating strikes) or block an incoming attack.

Once you are in your fighting stance, assess the threat as your assailant closes distance:

- is he or she armed, and if so, with what?
- can you retreat without exposing your back?
- is the person left or right handed?

Once you have answered these questions, select the appropriate defense and (if you are unable to retreat safely) a follow-up offense that will end the encounter quickly. No fight is predictable, so be prepared for anything.

Combinations

Like a good boxer, you must develop sets of blocks and strikes for any number of situations. However, you must not become predictable.

In many tournament fights, individuals generate reputations. For example, a fighter may be known for his knee strikes; in another case, a fighter may favor hand attacks. You do not want to develop such a reputation because it makes you predictable. In a street fight, predictability will put you at a severe disadvantage. Rather, you want your opponent to be confused. You want him or her off guard, not knowing from where your next block or strike will come from.

The following section presents sample combinations. After studying these, begin to create your own. You can become increasingly elaborate, generating situations in which you block, strike (and are thwarted), block again, strike and strike again, and block yet again.

Remember to vary your blocks and strikes, moving from crouching positions to side steps to striking from behind. Work to become an all-around fighter whose greatest strength is unpredictability.

A Word About Weapons

In a street fight, weapons most likely will be encountered. Indeed, this very book is designed around a socially accepted piece of wood that also can be used as a weapon.

Because of this reality, most of the combination examples are shown with both individuals brandishing weapons. Some weapons are more exotic than others, but the weapon types really do not matter.

The idea is to communicate the cane's effectiveness in defending against any kind of weapon, be it long, short, heavy, light, or exotic. Always keep in mind, however, that the wielder's skill in most cases will dictate the effectiveness of the weapon.

A later section specifically addresses one of the most common of hand-carried weapons, the knife. As for handguns, the cane is useless against them. As noted in the Bruce Lee film *Enter the Dragon*, anyone can pull a trigger.

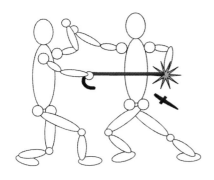

Remember that strikes can also serve as defense tools. For example, a strike to a hand holding a knife. is an effective defensive maneuver.

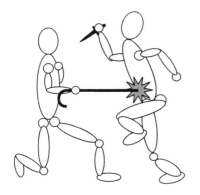

When developing combinations, make sure to vary your position. In this example, the cane fighter uses a kneeling position to strike from an unaccustomed angle. Such variation enhances your unpredictability in a fight.

Next to a handgun, a knife is perhaps the most popular weapon in a street fight. Do you have what it takes to ward off an assailant armed with such a weapon?

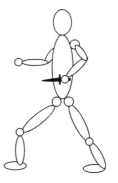

Sample Combinations

Combination 1

In this combination (see Figures 263-266), an assailant uses a pair of nun-chukus (a weapon developed in Okinawa) to generate a Horizontal Sweep power strike against the weak side of your head. To counter this strike, execute a Weak-Side Fencer's Block, using the Alive Hand to support the shaft.

While the assailant prepares a secondary strike, you can naturally flow from the block into a Fan Strike to the head. Even if the Fan Strike is blocked (the assailant could use the chain between the sticks to impede such as strike), you can follow up with a power strike, for the position is also suited for a Reverse Sweep Down power strike. Properly executed, such a power strike would get through even if the assailant mounted a proper defense.

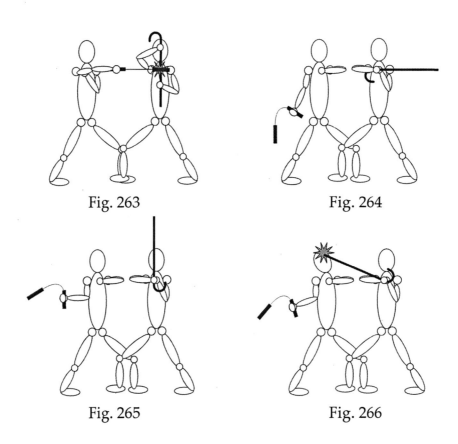

Fig. 263   Fig. 264

Fig. 265   Fig. 266

Combination 2

In this scenario (see Figures 267-272), you are surprised as an assailant pulls out a blade and prepares to thrust it into your chest or gut.

Because the attacker is so close, the combination uses a Weak-Side Offline Block. This avoids the thrusting blade (because you step to one side). The shaft is used to strike at the hand (if the blade is short) or at the weapon itself.

Even if the attacker does not drop the blade, striking it with full power deflects it downward, thus buying you time to create distance or counter with an offense, for example by flowing from the block into a Horn Strike to the Face.

By pushing this striking technique all the way through (cutting into a cheek with a downward slash), you can push the attacker forward, taking him or her off balance. From this position of advantage, you can end the fight with a power strike (Sweep Down) to the back of the opponent's head or neck.

To execute the power strike, after the jab, bring the cane around the back of your head, with the shaft's tip pointed down, as if wrapping it around your upper body. This flow will enable you to generate the momentum necessary for executing a truly powerful blow.

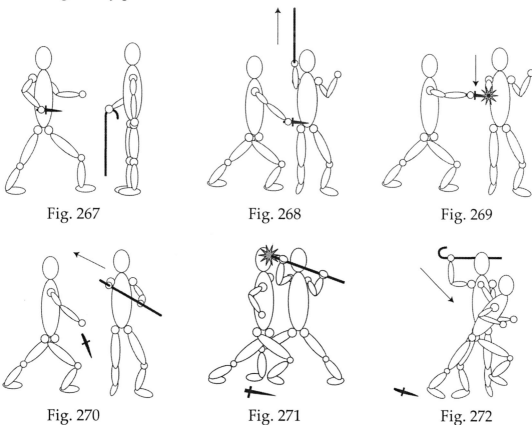

Fig. 267   Fig. 268   Fig. 269

Fig. 270   Fig. 271   Fig. 272

Combination 3

Some martial arts systems emphasize kicks because of their inherent power. However, most kicks place the individual in compromising positions, particularly if the defender is equally skilled and as fast. Combination 3 (see Figures 273-279) is designed to foil a kick to your strong side.

As the assailant begins to lift his or her knee to execute a kick, you can prepare to block it with a Strong-Side Mid-Level Block. Because the thigh muscle on a leg is extremely thick and resilient, use both hands to block the kick, with the Alive Hand open yet supporting the cane's shaft.

Before the opponent has a chance to put his or her leg down and attempt another technique, you should step in (creating a weak stance), at the same time driving the cane's shaft into the pelvis with a downward strike. Make sure to execute this strike with the end of the shaft to create maximum impact. Although not a powerful strike, it does generate some discomfort.

As the opponent tries to recover from this strike, you can bring the cane around his or her body, twisting the cane and driving the shaft into the assailant's groin. Executed properly, this strike is sure to create enough damage to end the fight; if not, you can follow-through with a power strike such as a Sweep Down to the back of the head or neck.

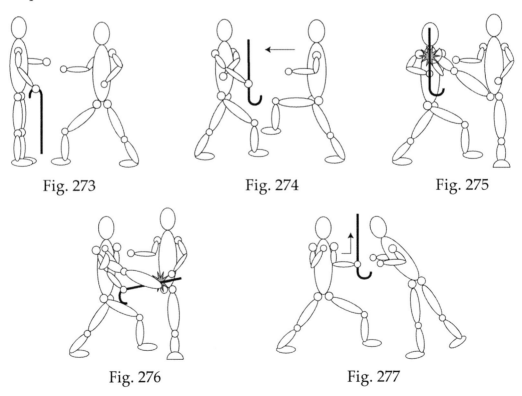

Fig. 273   Fig. 274   Fig. 275

Fig. 276   Fig. 277

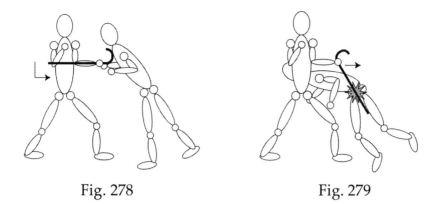

Fig. 278   Fig. 279

Combination 4

In this scenario (see Figures 280-284), an assailant with a baseball bat comes at you. As the assailant prepares for an overhead strike, you execute an Overhead Roof Block. This block is effective against heavy weapons, such as bats, pull cues, and iron pipes. However, it does open the body, so be prepared to follow up immediately after executing the block.

In this combination, you can push the bat to one side, using the cane's shaft to twist it down and away. Before the assailant can recover, thrust the cane's tip upward, jamming it under the opponent's chin. This strike is quite effective, and if executed with power, it can lead to the opponent's incapacitation. However, if the opponent somehow remains standing, you are in a position to follow-up with more thrusts to the body, particularly the chest, or by executing a Reverse Sweep Down power strike.

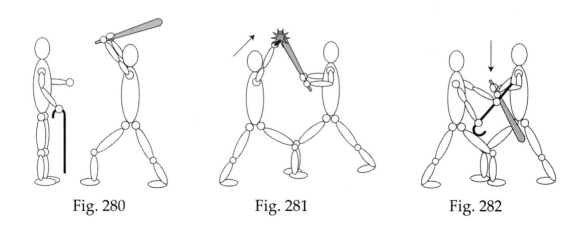

Fig. 280   Fig. 281   Fig. 282

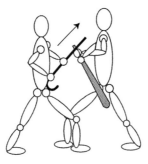

Fig. 283

Fig. 281

Combination 5

In this scenario, an attacker comes at you with an iron pipe. In an effort to catch you off guard, the assailant executes a weak-side horizontal strike to your strong side. To counter this move, execute a Strong-Side Down Parry Block. This striking block should deflect the power strike, but make sure to flick your wrist to generate power.

After executing the block, swing the cane as if generating a Weak-Side Down Parry Block, only drive the end of the cane's shaft into the inside of the opponent's knee.

If possible, strike the fleshy area behind the kneecap to create the most discomfort. Even if the opponent retains the weapon, the pain should serve as a temporary distraction.

To end the fight, step forward (creating a weak stance), stepping into the opponent's body. While doing this, drive the cane's horn into the assailant's groin. Pull up and away to create maximum discomfort.

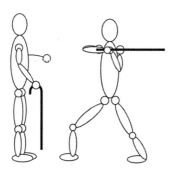

Fig. 285

Fig. 286

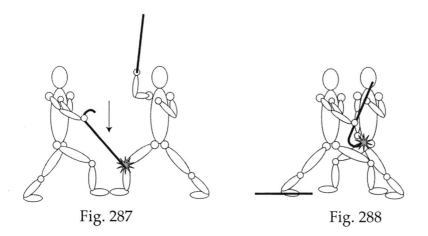

Fig. 287   Fig. 288

Combination 6

In this scenario (see Figures 289-296 below and overleaf), you begin with a modified neutral stance with the cane's horn pointing down and the crook's "butt" facing your opponent. Unlike walking or fighting sticks, the traditional cane's shape features a crook and horn that can be used to great effect, particularly if the horn ends with a vicious point (much like a shark's tooth).

As the assailant begins to rush at you, both hands extended, assume a weak-side stance then step off-line, maintaining the weak stance and placing most of your weight on your strong foot. As the opponent reaches for you, push his or her arms away with the cane, keeping the crook parallel to your body and the horn facing the assailant. Use the shaft to push away the arms so that the opponent is caught a little off-balance.

From this deflecting maneuver, you are positioned to bring the cane along the opponent's arms, driving the horn into his or her face. Tear the horn along the eyes, cheeks, and nose, ripping the cane all along the assailant's face and ear.

As the assailant reels in pain, flick the cane upward and bring it around the opponent's back, generating momentum as you do so. Acting as if you are going to strike a golf ball, drive the cane's horn into the back of the opponent's ankle, striking all the way through so that your opponent collapses to the ground. From this position you could use the horn to strike at the assailant's head, ribs, groin, or other soft body part. If the opponent is down for the count, then create distance and assess the scene again for any new dangers.

The key to this combination is the golfer-like swing to the ankle and follow-through sweep. This is a variation of a power strike, so if you are relatively weak, you may wish to use both hands when executing the maneuver. Remember, however, that the Alive Hand is often used to deflect any chance attacks, so if you use both hands, do so quickly and with all the power you can muster.

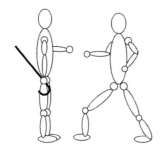

Fig. 289

Fig. 290

Fig. 291

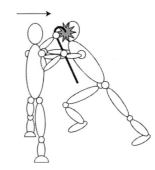

Fig. 292

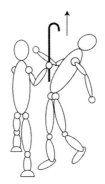

Fig. 293

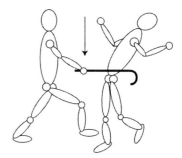

Fig. 294

Fig. 295

Fig. 296

RAISING CANE

Combination 7

This scenario shows how your body can supplement the cane. In the opening figure (Fig. 297, right), an assailant has flashed a blade but is wary of making a move. This hesitance happens often, particularly with individuals who are unskilled with bladed weapons.

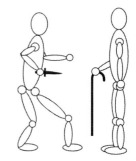

Fig. 297

Recognizing this reservation, you can elect to strike first. Moving into a strong stance, you can execute a Weak-Side Low-Level Strike to the knee and bring forward the Alive Hand, using your fingers to grasp the opponent's hair. The strike to the knee serves to generate shock, hopefully distracting the opponent so he or she does not strike with the blade. The knee you elect to strike is up to you—typically, the one that sticks out should be the one you should target.

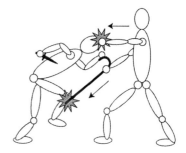

Fig. 298

Once you have hold of the hair (make sure your fingers have a solid grip, twisting them around the tresses if necessary), bring the opponent's head down, at the same time bringing your weak leg up. Jam the knee into the assailant's face, generating as much power as you can. While executing the knee strike, bring the cane up and away, with the shaft's tip pointing upward. Once you drive the knee into his or her face, drop your leg but hold the opponent's head down. Once you are on solid footing again (you will find yourself in a weak stance), bring down the cane, using the crook to strike at the back to the assailant's head or neck. At this point you can release the opponent and step away, if necessary using any of the Cinco Tiros should the opponent attempt to get up as you create distance.

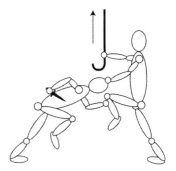

Fig. 299

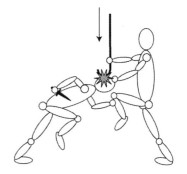

Fig. 300

Combination 8

In this scenario (see Figures 301-308), the assailant grabs you by the shirt, holding you in place while demanding your valuables. As his or her grip tightens, bring the cane up, weaving it through the abdomen and around so that the shaft rests on the assailant's outer arm and the tip points up.

Before the assailant can step away or execute a strike (at this point you are vulnerable to a knee to the groin), place the cane's shaft across both arms; concurrently, bring the Alive Hand to the tip-side of the cane and lock your fingers around the shaft. In effect you are forming a cross with your hands (Fig. 304). With both hands firmly on the cane, exert pressure on the assailant's arms (Fig.305).

Once you see an expression change on his or her face as a result of the discomfort (a grimace is likely), whip the opponent around your strong side, forcing the shaft down by pulling on both wrists. The pain and whipping motion should take the assailant off-balance (Fig. 306). Once he or she loses balance, release the shaft and bring the cane around to your weak side, holding the cane with both hands in a baseball stance (Fig. 307).

If the opponent tries to reach for your legs with his arms or kick out with either leg, you are in a position to execute Sweep Down power strike, which can be followed by a Reverse Sweep Down power strike. If the assailant attempts to stand, a solid thrust to the gut or groin will put a quick end to such a thought (Fig. 308).

If the opponent does not make a move quickly, take the opportunity to create distance and run to safety, all the time making sure that the assailant does not follow (always glance behind you). If he or she has the strength to do so, prepare for the next attack.

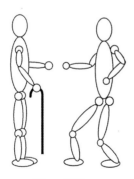

Fig. 301

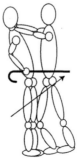

Fig. 302

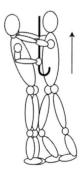

Fig. 303

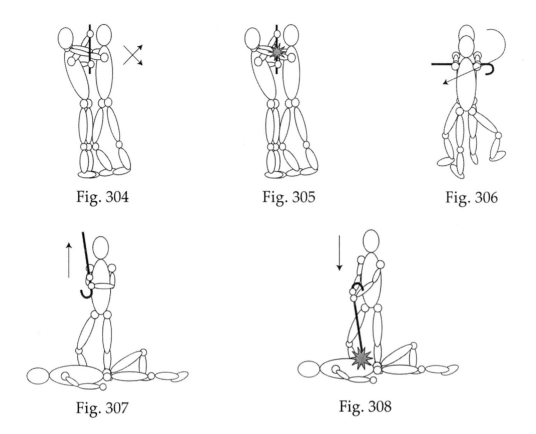

Fig. 304   Fig. 305   Fig. 306

Fig. 307   Fig. 308

Combination 9

We have already seen that fights are unpredictable. In this scenario (see Figures 309-314), the assailant brandishes an upturned broken bottle with a jagged edge. As the assailant thrusts forward in an attempt to cut your chest of face, you elect to execute a Strong-Side Step Offline Block, the cane's shaft striking at the top of the bottle while your body moves aside.

From this position, you flow naturally into a Strong-Side Axe Strike. As you execute this blow, the assailant uses both hands to block it, and although his fingers are damaged, he deflects the shaft away so that his or her head remains unharmed.

To open the upper body for another strike, you unleash the Alive Hand, thrusting it forward into the opponent's face. Attempt to poke the opponent's eyes, rake at his or her cheeks, or simply grab a collar or shirt front. This move will temporarily distract the assailant; he or she will move arms down and attempt to grab the Alive Hand.

In that instant, bring the cane across the opponent's face, using the horn to drive across the cheeks or temple. This strike to the head then enables you to step back and execute your choice of power strikes, hopefully ending the fight.

As this example shows, a fight may not end after the first few combinations, so be prepared to continue to fight until the opponent is subdued. Make sure to practice the both sets so that you develop the ability to create combinations for every contingency. The best way to end an encounter is to use the Cinco Tiros, so once an opportunity presents itself, be prepared to use the power strikes.

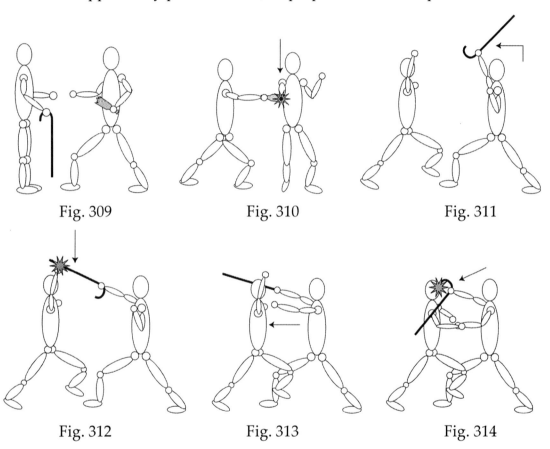

Fig. 309   Fig. 310   Fig. 311

Fig. 312   Fig. 313   Fig. 314

Combination 10

In this final combination, you face an opponent wielding a stick (such as a pool cue) that is longer than your cane. This means you must be ready to close distance and thus neutralize the assailant's weapon (remember, the tip and surrounding area are the most effective pieces of any stick weapon).

In this scenario (Figures 315-320), the assailant executes a Horizontal Sweep power strike to the head, which you counter with an Closing the Umbrella block, bringing the cane up enough to counter the blow. Having impeded the strike, continue with the block's flow until the cane's shaft is perpendicular over your head. Now swing the cane so that the shaft points away from the back of your head (Fig. 317) and step forward (Fig. 318), nullifying the opponent's ability to strike effectively.

Before the opponent can prepare a defense or strike again, quickly swing the cane around your weak side, using the shaft to strike at the opponent's temple. Using a helicopter motion, swing the cane around your head and strong side, striking the opponent's other temple. Do this twice if you have the opportunity. If not, bring the cane around your head and generate a power strike to the head, ribs, or knee. You could even execute a few well-placed thrusts to the chest, gut, or groin.

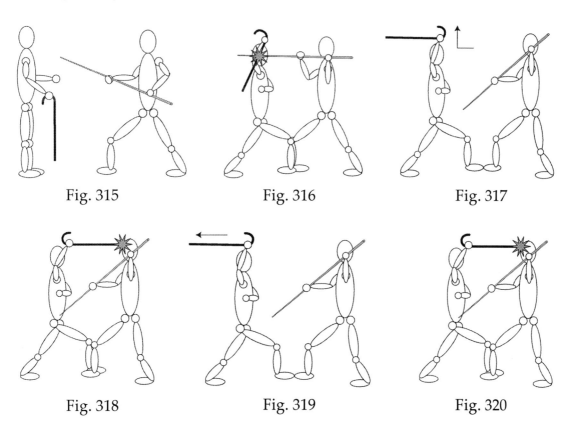

Fig. 315   Fig. 316   Fig. 317

Fig. 318   Fig. 319   Fig. 320

Using the Alive Hand

As you have seen in some of the strikes, blocks, and combinations, the Alive Hand can come into play as a secondary weapon. As Filipino Kalistas or Escrimadores progress in their art, they began to develop Siniwali, which means that they are equally adept with both hands—this then progresses to using two weapons concurrently, such as two sticks, a stick and short sword (like a machete), a stick and knife, and two short swords (the most dangerous art of all). This is a difficult skill to acquire, sometimes requiring years on intense development.

For the purposes of fighting with the cane, Siniwali plays only a minor role. Once you have cultivated an ease with the strike and block sets and have begun to develop effective combinations (through practicing fights with a partner), you can begin to incorporate the use of the Alive Hand into every facet of a fight.

Alive Hand Placement

As stated in the Basics section of this book, the Alive Hand's traditional purpose is to protect the heart. Therefore, the hand rests on the chest, palm against flesh, with the elbow tucked into the rib cage. This posture is the Alive Hand's defensive mode (Fig. 321). In this default position, you present to the opponent flesh and muscle and very few blood vessels. If you are struck or cut along this arm or hand, you should be able to continue the fight.

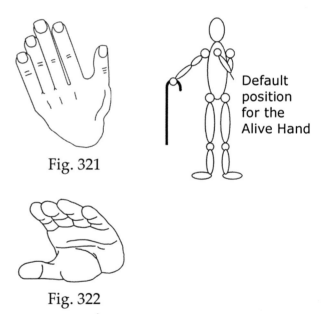

Fig. 321

Default position for the Alive Hand

Fig. 322

A key idea of this self-defense system is to exploit whatever opportunities an assailant presents to you. For example, if an opponent sticks out his or her knee during a fight, zero in on that target and take it out. If an opponent opens his or her hand while twirling a stick, strike at the stick or hand and send the shaft flying into the air.

As you practice creating combinations, you will notice opportunities to strike with the Alive Hand. When such an opportunity presents itself, you must act immediately and decisively.

Figure 322 shows the position of the Alive Hand in an offensive mode. When you are ready to use the hand, bring it off the chest, turn it so that the back of the hand rests off the chest and the palm is out, and close the fingers and thumb so that the hand assumes a C-like shape.

Figures 323-329 show how the Alive Hand flows in a typical strike. Figures 323-325 demonstrate a simple Strong-Side Low-Level strike to an opponent's knee. Once you have completed the movements associated with this strike, you may see an opponent turn to one side and use his or her arms in an attempt to deflect the blow, thus leaving his or her strong side open and vulnerable.

To take advantage of this, bring the Alive Hand into an offensive position (Fig. 326) and quickly thrust it forward (Fig. 327), reaching for whatever target is available. Once you have accomplished your goal (or if you miss the opportunity), retract the Alive Hand as soon as possible (Fig. 328) so that it in turn does not become a target.

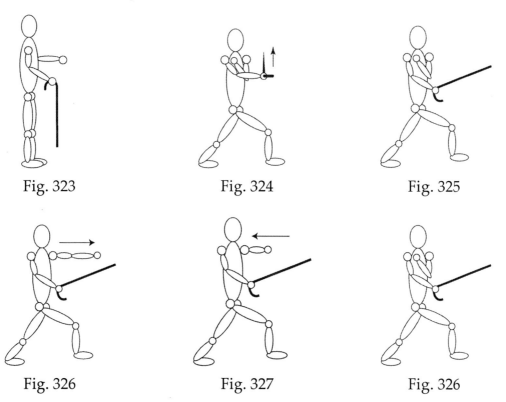

Fig. 323   Fig. 324   Fig. 325

Fig. 326   Fig. 327   Fig. 326

The following subsections show some of the follow-up techniques that you can implement following such a strike.

Strike to the Opponent's Weak-Side Knee

After successfully striking the opponent's weak-side knee (Fig. 330), you take a short step in, the Alive Hand reaching out and taking hold of a chunk of hair (Fig. 331). You then drive the cane's shaft into the groin (Fig. 332) and follow up with a power strike if necessary.

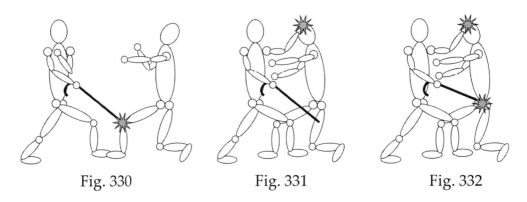

Fig. 330   Fig. 331   Fig. 332

Strike to the Opponent's Strong-Side Knee

After successfully striking an opponent's strong-side knee (Fig. 333), thrust the Alive Hand forward (Fig. 334), pushing the opponent off his or her feet (Fig. 335). Even if the opponent does not fall down, he or she will need a second or two to regain balance, at which time you can follow up with any of the Cinco Tiros power strikes. If the opponent does fall down, you are in a position to prepare for the power strikes as well (Fig. 336).

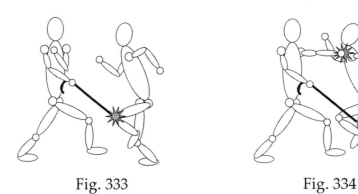

Fig. 333   Fig. 334

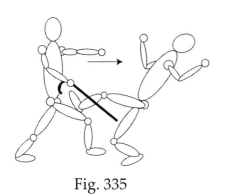

Fig. 335   Fig. 336

Blocked Knee Strike

The opponent uses a traditional martial arts block to counter your strike, in this case to his or her weak side (Fig. 337). As he or she attempts to follow up with a strike (or perhaps create distance), reach out and grab the opponent's hair (Fig. 338) and follow through with a knee (Fig 339) and a strike to the head with the crook (Fig. 340).

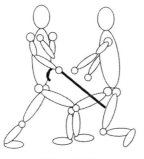

Fig. 337

Fig. 338

Fig. 339

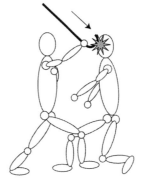

Fig. 340

Blocked Knee Strike (Variations)

The opponent uses a traditional martial arts block to counter your strike (Fig. 341). As he or she attempts to follow up with a strike, thrust the Alive Hand forward and (1) use the index and middle fingers to poke at the eyes (Fig. 342) or (2) keep the hand in the C-configuration and use the palm to strike the chin or nose (Fig. 343).

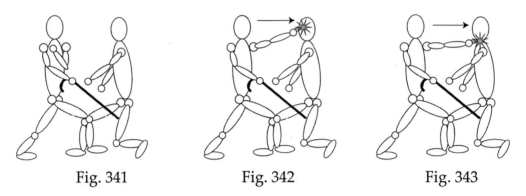

Fig. 341   Fig. 342   Fig. 343

The Quick Flick

When facing an experienced fighter who also happens to be quick, you may not have time to move the Alive Hand from the defensive to the offensive posture. If the opponent bocks the strike (Fig. 344) and pushes in quickly (Fig. 345), simply thrust the Alive Hand out, palm to you, and flick the wrist, thus letting the fingers strike the assailant's face (Figs. 346 and 347).

Relax your fingers as much as possible when striking—it is as if you are slapping somebody's face, but your are doing so with "broken" fingers. Although this flicking motion only causes temporary discomfort and confusion, it will enable you to follow through with a power strike.

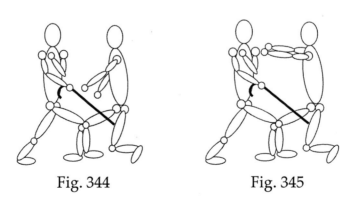

Fig. 344   Fig. 345

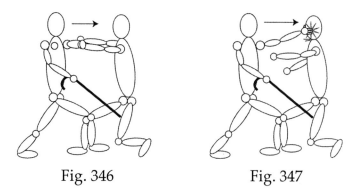

Fig. 346   Fig. 347

Opening the Body

By opening the body, I mean striking anything that presents itself. If an opponent sticks out a foot, take out the toes, ankle, and knee. If an opponent charges in headfirst, take out the head and neck.

If an opponent keeps a hand static or thrusts forward with a knife, you should strike at the fingers, the wrist, or the weapon itself (as shown in Fig. 348). Remember, pain and discomfort contribute to the psychology of a fight.

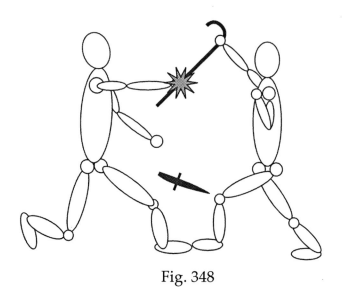

Fig. 348

Closing Distance

Under some circumstances, you may wish to end a fight quickly and decisively. In such cases, you should be prepared to be the aggressor. The first step in gaining the upper hand is to stop a potential attack before the opponent can execute it. To accomplish this goal, you will need to close distance immediately.

Figure 349 shows the footwork necessary for closing distance. As you can see, the movement consists of five principal steps. From the first step, pivot toward your weak side, taking one step forward (a weak stance). From here, pivot to your strong side, taking two quick steps forward, then pivoting so that you face forward once again, assuming a strong stance as you strike. Practice this move and increase the speed once you are comfortable with it. Remember, you want to execute this move as quickly as possible.

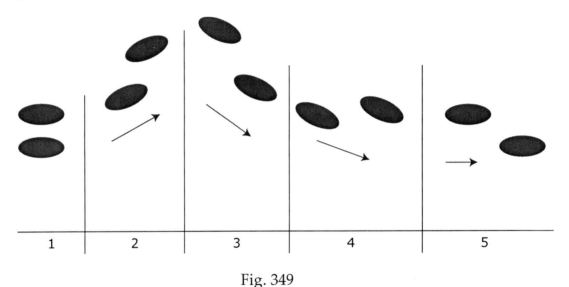

Fig. 349

While executing this footwork, your upper body will be moving as well. Figures 350 to 355 show what cane movements you will make while executing the footwork. Figure 350 shows the neutral stance. As you pivot to the weak side, begin to execute the Opening the Umbrella Block (Fig. 351). As you bound toward the strong side, open the umbrella, in effect blocking any blow from above and also feigning a strike (Fig. 353). As you straighten out (using your weak side to jam the opponent's strong side) so that you are face to face with your opponent, thrust the cane's tip forward, striking as many times as possible before your opponent creates distance or he or she is incapacitated.

RAISING CANE

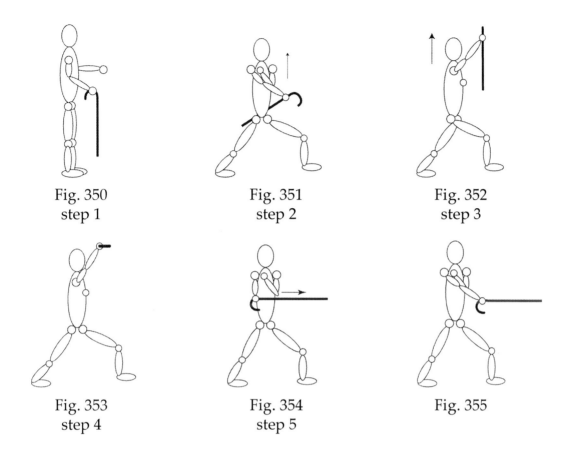

Fig. 350
step 1

Fig. 351
step 2

Fig. 352
step 3

Fig. 353
step 4

Fig. 354
step 5

Fig. 355

Clearing the Air

During its turbulent history, the Philippine Islands have been conquered many times. During some of these times, the fighting arts went underground, sometimes disguised as elaborate dances. From these dances the Filipino fighting arts gained a certain beauty and finesse.

As you advance with the cane, you may wish to incorporate some of the more fundamental stick twirls, particularly those that can be executed by holding onto the cane's crook (see Fig. 356).

In the Flexibility Strikes section of this book, you learned how to execute forward and reverse figure-eight techniques known as redondos. In this section, this technique is expanded, with the resultant redondos much faster and more menacing.

Fig. 356

This fundamental twirling techniques is particularly effective at "clearing the air" when an opponent wishes to close distance against you. By executing this figure-eight technique, the speed and force of the moves alone will either keep the assailant back or the shaft will strike whatever the opponent presents (such as a hand, knee, even a chin).

The Twirling "X"

This technique consists of a Strong-Side Redondo and Weak-Wide Redondo, only these are executed by holding onto the cane's crook. Make sure to keep a loose grip on the crook as you spin the cane's shaft, but also make sure to tighten the grip at any time so that you do not lose your weapon.

Figures 357 through 359 show a Strong-Side Redondo. As you execute this move, you hand should be palm up, with the thumb tucked in. Rotate the wrist slightly to build the shaft's momentum.

Figure 360 is a transition move to the weak side. At this point, the hand twists so that it points palm down, which in turn naturally forces the cane to spin toward your weak side (Fig. 361) and downward (Fig. 362).

From this position, simply flick the wrist to bring the shaft along your weak side (Fig. 363) and upward, at which point you twist your wrist, once again having the hand point palm up (Fig. 364).

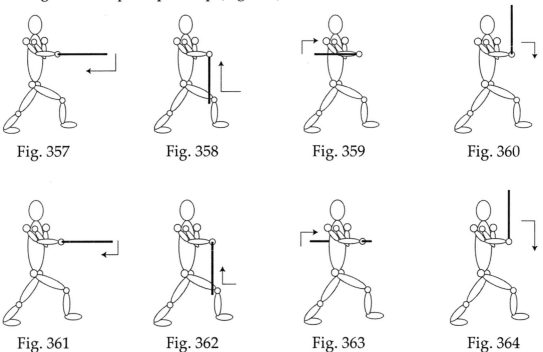

Fig. 357   Fig. 358   Fig. 359   Fig. 360

Fig. 361   Fig. 362   Fig. 363   Fig. 364

Practice this technique slowly at first, paying particular attention to the wrist's twisting motion. As you become more comfortable with the movement, increase the speed.

Once you develop proficiency with this technique, begin to experiment with the twirling motion. For example, twirl the shaft above your head by twisting your wrist and pushing the shaft like a helicopter blade.

Disarming

Disarming techniques are often flowery and exciting to watch, but rarely are they effective. The reason for this is that most techniques involve an opponent who, once he or she executes a strike, remains static long enough for you to execute an involved disarm.

In a real fight, you are rarely afforded such a luxury. The following sections provide a few simple and effective disarming examples. Use these techniques sparingly. Once an opponent realizes that you are executing disarming techniques, he or she will be on guard for more and you will be at a severe disadvantage.

Retaining Your Weapon

Before learning to disarm and opponent, you must learn to retain your own weapon. The following techniques are designed to help you counter an opponent's attempt to render your weapon useless.

Counter Against Wrist Grab

If an opponent surmises that your cane can be used as a weapon, he or she will probably attempt to disarm you immediately. In this example, an assailant has grabbed you by the wrist with the intent of keeping the cane in position (Fig. 365).

As this happens, move into a strong stance and bring the cane's shaft around your strong side (Fig. 366) and over toward the weak side (Fig. 367) until it lies across the opponent's wrist(s) or upper forearm(s), as shown in Fig. 368.

At this point, bring the Alive Hand over so that it grasps the shaft, palm down, against the opponent's wrist. Make sure you have a solid grip on the shaft so that the opponent cannot drive the cane's shaft upward into your face.

Using both hands, press the shaft down onto the opponent's wrist(s), crouching as needed. Drive his or her wrist down so that the fingers either release or the wrist breaks.

Once the opponent releases your cane, follow-up with a knee strike or use the cane to execute a power strike, such as a Sweep Up.

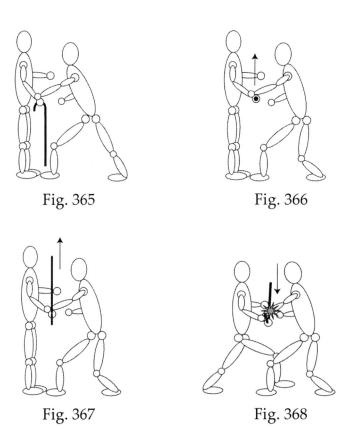

Fig. 365

Fig. 366

Fig. 367

Fig. 368

Releasing the Dragon's Tale

It is basic human instinct to reach out and grab anything thrown at you. Therefore, expect your opponent to reach and out grab your cane at any given opportunity.

When you are confronted (Fig. 369), you elect to defend yourself, executing a strike or a thrust with your handy cane. However, as you strike, your opponent catches the cane's shaft with his or her hand (Fig. 370).

In this example, the assailant has grabbed your cane with the hand palm down (Fig. 371), although this technique works equally with a palm-up grab.

Rather than engage in a fruitless tug of war, push the shaft upward, driving the tip so that it rests against the opponent's wrist (Fig. 372). As the opponent's hand is pulled downward, wrap the tip area so that it comes around the wrist (Fig. 373). At this point, push the shaft down. Continue to push down, forcing the opponent's hand and wrist to contort so much that he or she has no choice but to let go (Fig. 374).

If you have the opportunity, you may place your hand on the opponent's hand (Fig. 375). As you execute the technique, keep the hand in place (Fig. 376), so that as the cane's shaft is twisted, you force your opponent to the ground.

Once you have freed your weapon, make sure to follow-up with another strike, preferably a power technique so that the opponent does not have the opportunity to catch the cane's shaft again.

Fig. 371

Fig. 372

Fig. 373

Fig. 374

Fig. 375

Fig. 376

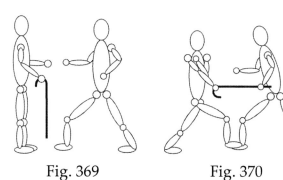

Fig. 369   Fig. 370

Fulcrum Strike

In some instances, an assailant may grab the cane's shaft with both hands. If this happens, do not engage in a tug of war—it will be fruitless and in that time the opponent may achieve one of two things.

Firstly, he or she may win the tug-of-war, in which case he or she have use of your weapon. Secondly, the opponent may try something else (like stomping a foot, kicking or sweeping a knee, or punching your face), thus forcing you to defend against such a move. In the process, you will lose your weapon.

Once an opponent grabs your cane with both hands (Fig. 377), take a few steps in and also grab the cane with both hands (Fig. 378), placing the Alive Hand in a palm-down grip. The opponent may now believe that you are about to engage in a pulling match, but instead you will use the assailant's grip as a fulcrum for a surprise strike.

As quickly as possible, shift your weapon hand into a palm-down grip and at the same time push the crook upward and into the opponent's face (Fig. 379). Use the crook to strike (Fig. 380), and if possible, twist the shaft so you can strike with the horn, perhaps following up by raking the horn across the face or around the neck, with the latter move easily leading to a takedown.

Even if an opponent realizes that you are using his or her grip as a fulcrum and disengages before you strike, you achieve a victory in that the cane's shaft is free. If this happens, be prepared to follow-up with a barrage of strikes, preferably a combination of either set of Cinco Tiros.

Fig. 377

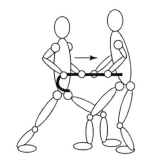

Fig. 378

Fig. 379

Fig. 380

Under-the-Arm Throw

When striking an opponent's weak side, it is possible for him or her to "catch" such a strike under the arm (Fig. 381). By turning quickly to toward the weak side, the assailant can wrench the cane away, leaving you vulnerable. Even if this does not happen, the opponent has at the minimum rendered you weapon ineffective.

Once an opponent traps the cane's shaft, quickly step forward, moving the weapon hand up and wrapping the Alive Hand around the other side of the shaft (Fig. 382). Make sure both hands have a solid grip.

Before the opponent has a chance to follow-up with a move of his or her own, pull the shaft toward you, and at the same time, throw a knee into the opponent's groin or gut (Fig. 383). Your opponent should double over a little. If necessary, follow-up with a second knee to achieve this effect.

After softening this vulnerable area, resume solid footing and pull the opponent through your weak side, literally throwing him or her to the ground (Fig. 384). When the opponent loses his or her footing, release the cane and let him or her fall to the ground.

Once the opponent is on the ground, you may elect to follow-up with a thrust to the groin or face. At this point you are in a superior position in the fight and it most likely is over.

Fig. 381

Fig. 382

Fig. 383

Fig. 384

Disarming an Opponent

Use these techniques only if given an opportunity! Never forget: an opponent does not remain static for long; therefore, be sure to practice these techniques so that they become second nature. Use the techniques sparingly—mixing a disarming technique among a barrage of blocks and strikes will catch an opponent off guard. In the end, you will not only to win a fight but also end up with his or her weapon.

In this section, I will present five disarms. Of these five, two are very basic. Practice these first two often—their simplicity will enable you to use them easily at an appropriate moment during a fight. The remaining three, all of which use a snake metaphor, are more complex and require much more practice.

Trap and Smash

In the scenario shown below, the assailant prepares to assault with a stick such as a baseball bat or club (Fig. 385). As the opponent strikes, you block (a mid-level block is most effective) and catch the stick under your arm (Fig. 386). At the same time, you bring the cane up so that the tip points upward.

Having temporarily trapped the assailant's weapon, you then use the Alive Hand to secure it and at the same time bring the cane's horn down on the opponent's wrist (Fig. 387). Bring the strike through the wrist and at the same time twist your body, wrenching the weapon away (Fig. 388).

If you allow your opponent a chance to recover, he or she could (for example) move in to establish a bear hug or other hold and then proceed to execute an effective grappling maneuver, such as a half-nelson or an elbow strike to your chest. Deny this opportunity by following up with a power strike to the head. Even if this strike misses, you will have created distance. Disarmed, the attacker may even consider flight. If he or she elects to continue the fight, you now have access to both weapons.

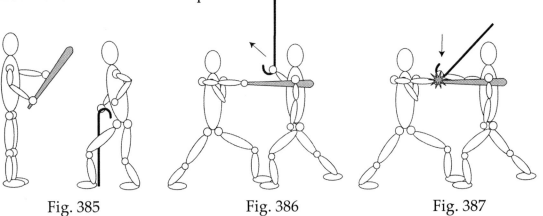

Fig. 385   Fig. 386   Fig. 387

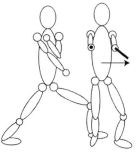

Fig. 388   Fig. 389

Block and Strike

This is a simple variation of the previous disarm. As the assailant prepares to strike (Fig. 390), you elect to use Weak-Side Offline Block (Fig. 391). If the opponent retains his or her weapon, reach down with the Alive Hand and grab the end of the shaft (Fig. 392).

As the assailant attempts to wrench away his or her weapon, use the Alive Hand to push down on it while bringing the weapon arm up (Fig. 393). Then bring down the cane's shaft onto the assailant's hand, using the edge to strike at the fingers or wrist (Fig. 394). From this point, simply pull the weapon away and follow-up with a power strike to the head (Fig. 395).

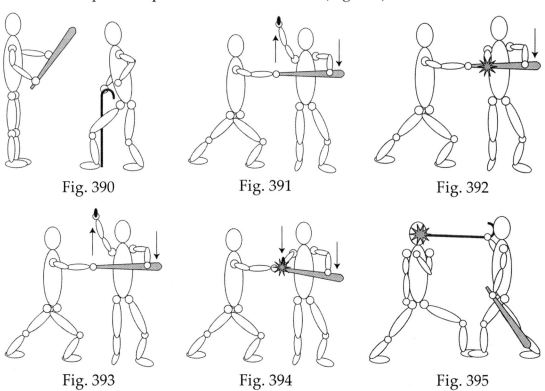

Fig. 390   Fig. 391   Fig. 392

Fig. 393   Fig. 394   Fig. 395

Defanging the Snake

This is a dangerous disarm, but one that you may wish to consider when facing an assailant armed with a blade. As you and the opponent square off (Fig. 396), be prepared for a thrust or an attack to your weak side. If the opponent elects to slash at your weak side (an attack above the gut and into any body part, including the face, shoulder, chest, and gut), execute an Opening the Umbrella Block (Fig. 397), using the cane's shaft to intercept the opponent's wrist or forearm and not the blade (Fig. 398).

Once you have blocked the weapon, the opponent will quickly strike again, so before he or she can do this, swing the shaft toward your strong side, bringing the tip upward (Fig. 399). As the opponent prepares to strike (most likely with another slash, this time toward your strong side, or with a thrust into your chest or neck), bring the cane down, using the crook to strike at the opponent's outside wrist area (Fig. 400). Using all the power you can muster, sweep the cane downward, if possible, catching the blade's guard or even the blade itself in the process. Wrench the blade away, or at the minimum, strike the wrist so hard that the fingers loosen.

If you have an understanding of brachial stuns and know how to execute them, then use the cane's crook to strike at the forearm's most vulnerable area. *Do this only if you understand such techniques!* Otherewise, go for the wrist and the blade itself.

Draw the shaft downward. As the opponent recovers from the sting, naturally follow through with a thrust to his or her chest or gut (Fig. 401). Thrust as many times as necessary, or after several key thrusts, back away and execute a few follow-up power strikes in the process.

This technique is dangerous because as you strike the opponent's wrist to disarm, there is a chance that the blade will cut your own hand. Be ready for this. Any cut will sting and bleed: do not allow your concentration to waver. Follow through the technique, making sure to bring the cane's shaft all the way through so that you at least cause discomfort and are ready to follow through with a thrust and power strikes.

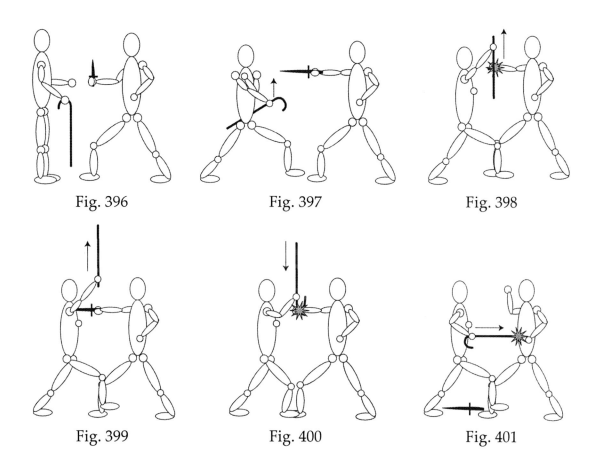

Fig. 396

Fig. 397

Fig. 398

Fig. 399

Fig. 400

Fig. 401

Weaving the Snake

When facing off against an assailant with a stick (piece of wood, crowbar, iron pipe, etc.), you may an opportunity to disarm, particularly if the opponent's weapon is heavy and unwieldy. As you face off (Fig 402), watch the opponent's handling of the weapon. If he or she is unsure or if the weapon is heavy, prepare to execute a disarming technique once the attack comes.

As the assailant strikes (by swinging or thrusting at your weak side) execute a Weak-Side Step Offline Block, striking at the weapon (Fig. 403). If the opponent retains the weapon, you may wish to continue the disarming motion. To do so, grab the end of the striking stick with the Alive Hand and at the same time begin to weave the cane's shaft over the opponent's stick (Fig. 404).

As the cane is woven under the opponent's wrist, pull down on the captured shaft (Fig. 405). Push the cane's shaft up and pull the captured stick down, forcing the opponent's hand open (Fig. 406). Wrench the captured stick away and continue pushing the cane upward. You are now in a position to use either or both sticks to follow-up with thrusts or other combinations (Fig. 407).

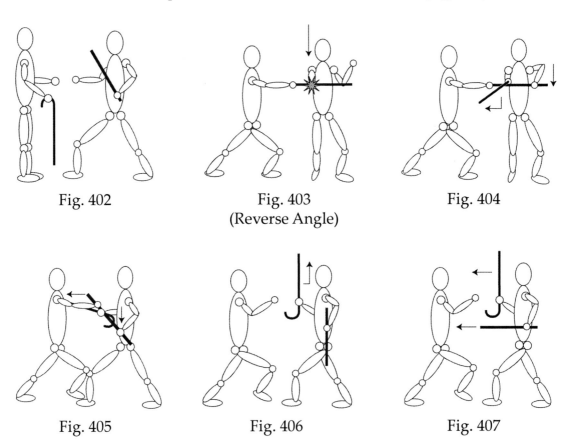

Fig. 402

Fig. 403
(Reverse Angle)

Fig. 404

Fig. 405

Fig. 406

Fig. 407

Snake Weaves and Bites

When an attacker armed with a stick goes for your knee or ankle (Fig. 408), you can deflect the blow by using a Weak-Side Broom Block (Fig. 409). Once you have deflected the strike, push the shaft forward, keeping your palm facing the opponent's stick (Fig. 410). Using the cane's shaft like a snake, weave it around the assailant's weapon until yours points upward (Fig. 411).

Once the cane's tip points upward, step into the opponent, assuming a side-step strong stance. At the same time, bring the cane's shaft onto the assailant's weapon or wrist (Fig. 412). As you strike this delicate area, use the Alive Hand to grab the assailant's weapon As you pivot away from the opponent, wrench the weapon from his or her grasp by using the Alive Hand and the underarm of the weapon hand (Fig. 413).

Your back is now vulnerable: before your assailant can attack it, strike with an elbow (Fig. 414) or (if you have the opportunity) use the cane to strike with a backhanded blow. Quickly whirl around so that you once again face the opponent. With his weapon now yours, strike at his or her head with both weapons (Fig. 415).

As you can see, disarms can be quite elaborate, yet if you can pull one off, you can strike with impunity. Remember, however, to apply the simple disarms before attempting a more complex one. Most importantly, never forget that disarms often fail, so be prepared to follow-through quickly with other techniques or to create distance.

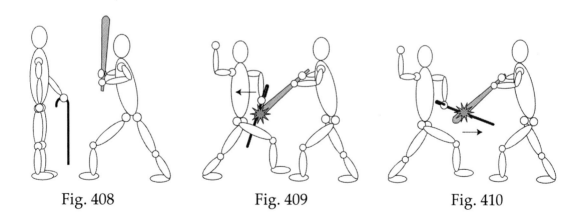

Fig. 408   Fig. 409   Fig. 410

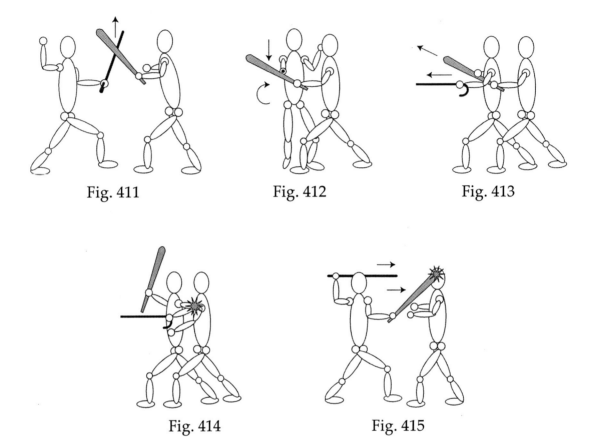

Fig. 411

Fig. 412

Fig. 413

Fig. 414

Fig. 415

Part Five
Training and Conditioning

Introduction

To become adept with the introductory techniques presented in this book, you must be willing to set aside many hours of practice. Unfortunately, many beginning practitioners quit training long before they acquire the skills. The main reason for giving up is that these techniques require strong wrists, arms, shoulders, and back.

In a fight, you must be able to block and strike continuously, creating an array of combinations and not once stopping to take a breath. Each strike must be delivered as if it were your last.

This section provides exercises designed to strengthen your forearms and wrists. These two body parts are crucial for manipulating the cane as a self-defense weapon.

As with any exercise program, make sure you consult a physician to ascertain your physical condition before you begin.

Alphabet Soup

This training technique can enhance your ability to manipulate the cane and thus create a variety of combinations. This tool also helps strengthen your arms and wrists and augments your flexibility.

Assume a strong stance, your weapon hand at the ready with the cane you intend to use on the street. Using the shaft's tip as a pencil, write out the alphabet using strike motions. Go as far into the alphabet as you can, then switch to the weak hand and do the exercise again.

An example of the strikes that can be used to create a letter "O" appears below, with the letter "A" on the opposite page.

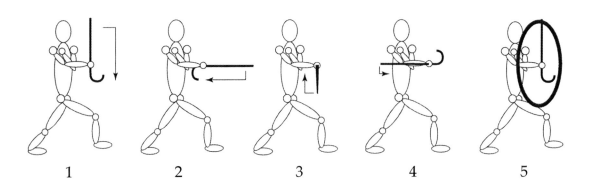

| 1 | 2 | 3 | 4 | 5 |

Building the Letter "A"

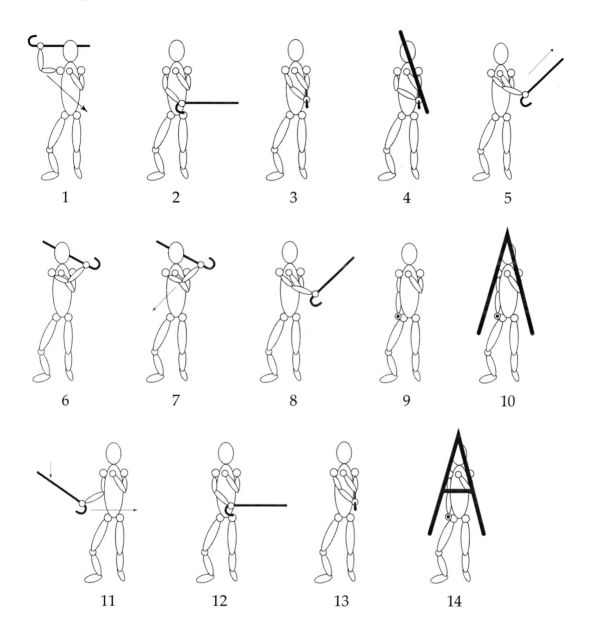

1   2   3   4   5

6   7   8   9   10

11   12   13   14

The cane requires strong wrists and joints. Start slowly and practice until you are comfortable with the techniques before working on power.

Begin these exercises slowly to become comfortable with the movement. As you build speed and force, you will build power.

Heavy Bag Work

To develop power in your strikes, I advise using a heavy bag such as those used by boxers. If you can, purchase a padded stick (martial arts stores and catalogs usually have them) to use on the bag so that it can take more strikes. Remember to make each strike count—hit as hard as you possibly can.

Although such a stick lacks a crook and horn, practice the strikes and blocks as if these assets were present—remember, the cane is more than just a stick.

Using a heavy bag will teach you power; moreover, it will show you that a loose grip negatively affects the stability of the stick and reduces the resultant power.

If you have a loose grip, the stick may fly out of your hand during a strike. Do not forget this lesson; imagine the consequences of losing the weapon during a fight.

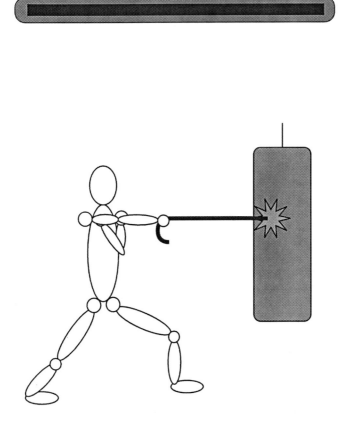

This schematic of a padded stick shows a plastic center (black) surrounded by soft foam (gray). These sticks are commonly found in martial arts supply shops or in specialty catalogs, particularly those catering to Filipino martial arts.

Heavy bag workouts enable you to develop power. Once you have developed power, you and a sparring-partner can use foam sticks and body armor to practice real-world fights.

Weight Room Exercises

The following exercises are designed to strengthen the forearms and wrists. As with any exercise program, make sure that you are in good health. In addition, make sure you understand how to operate exercise equipment safely.

Preacher Bench Curl.
This traditional exercise strengthens the biceps and forearms. A curling bar isolates these muscles, and the preacher bench ensures that you do not use your shoulders or roll your body during the exercise. You also can use two dumbbells to execute this exercise.

Grasping the bar so that the palms of your hands and the inside of your forearms face outward (Fig. 416), bring the bar up, making sure not to arch you back or lift your butt off the seat (Fig. 417). Curl the bar until your palms and inside of your forearms face inward (Fig. 418).

If you feel your back arch, tighten your gut and leg muscles to regain balance.

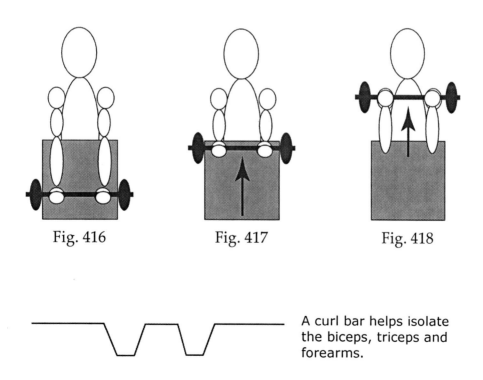

Fig. 416   Fig. 417   Fig. 418

A curl bar helps isolate the biceps, triceps and forearms.

Reverse Curl

For this exercise, you can use a triceps curl bar or a straight bar, depending on your overall strength and needs. Grasping the bar with the your palms facing the preacher bench—if you extended your fingers, they would point down (Fig. 419)—bring the bar up, making sure not to arch you back or lift your butt off the seat (Fig. 420).

Curl the bar until your palms and inside of your forearms face outward (Fig. 421). Keep your wrists straight. Do not allow them to bend during the exercise.

If you feel your back arch, tighten your gut and leg muscles to regain balance.

Wrist Curl

For this exercise, you can use the edge of the preacher bench or another suitable surface. Place your elbows on the surface and grasp the bar with your hands' palms facing you (Fig. 422).

From this position, slowly ease the weight down, using your wrists to control its descent. Do this until the wrists lock naturally (Fig. 423). Slowly pull the bar back toward you, returning to the starting position (Fig. 424).

Do not roll the bar. Make each movement fluid, stopping at each point for a second or two. This type of resistance increases strength and flexibility. For a full effect, reverse the position of your hands so that the palms face away from you and do the exercise again.

Dumbell Twist

Take a dumbbell and extend your arm so that it hangs from the shoulder (Fig. 425). Keeping the arm straight, slowly rotate the dumbbell clockwise, using only the wrist. Stop the motion when the wrist no longer can twist (Fig. 426).

Pause for a two-count and bring the dumbbell to the starting position (Fig. 427). Now rotate the dumbbell counterclockwise, once again stopping when the wrist no longer can twist (Fig. 428).

A clockwise and counterclockwise twist equals one repetition. Remember to twist the dumbbell slowly—do not create momentum because it detracts from the exercise.

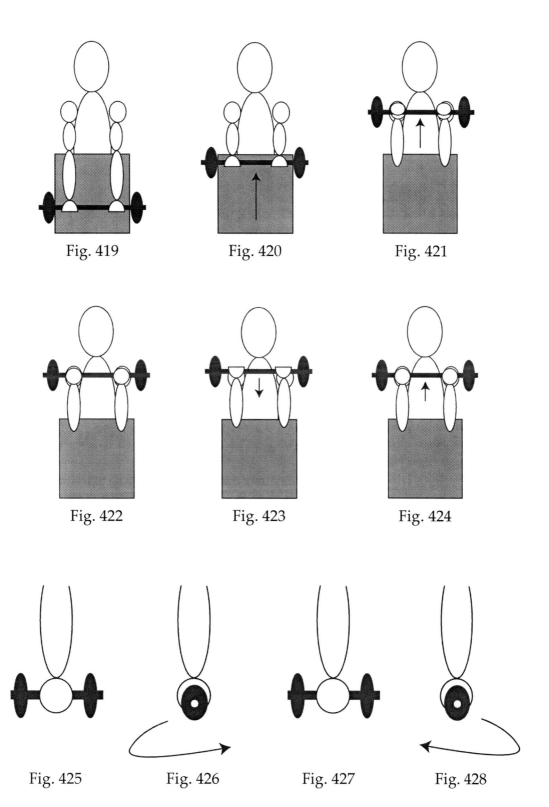

Fig. 419

Fig. 420

Fig. 421

Fig. 422

Fig. 423

Fig. 424

Fig. 425

Fig. 426

Fig. 427

Fig. 428

Body Exercises

Not every practitioner has access to a gym and its strength-training equipment, so in this section I will discuss exercises that require only the human body. In some instances, a relatively inexpensive and easily storable piece of equipment will be used.

Evolving Pushups
Pushups are excellent for upper-body and wrist strength. In this section, I provide pushup techniques that become increasingly difficult as you become stronger.

Standard Pushup
The basic pushup, in which the arms are either inside or outside the shoulders, is designed to strengthen the chest, shoulders, or upper arms (biceps/triceps).

Triangle Pushup
When you can do approximately 50 pushups in under a minute, you can begin to incorporate a more advanced pushup. Remember, this advanced technique will place more tension on your wrists, so make sure to slowly integrate this pushup into your routine.

To execute a triangle pushup, assume a standard pushup posture, only this time bring your hands together so that they form a pyramid (Fig. 429). From this position, with the index fingers and thumbs touching, execute the pushups, making sure to maintain balance.

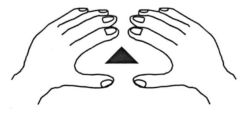

Fig. 429

Fist Pushup

Also known as the knuckle pushup, the fist pushup is a basic pushup performed with both hands balled into fists. The palms face each other.

Spider Pushup

An extremely advanced pushup, the spider pushup requires extreme strength, particularly in the fingers. Figure 430 shows the hand's placement when executing this pushup.

Fig. 430

Gripping a Ball or Squeezing Putty

Holding a tennis or tension ball (available at most sporting goods stores) in the palm of either hand (Fig. 431), wrap the fingers and thumb around it and squeeze as hard as you can. Relax you hand and squeeze again.

After some practice, you may wish to exercise each finger independently, using each to squeeze down on the ball. This exercise not only increases forearm and finger strength, it also enhances finger and wrist flexibility.

If you want something a bit more flexible to squeeze, you can buy some strengthening putty. This material can be found in stores catering to weightlifters.

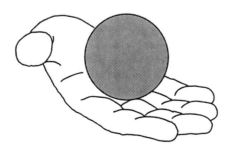

Fig. 431

Muscle-Building System

Because forearms and wrist strength and flexibility are crucial to cane manipulation, you should execute these body exercises daily. However, you can incorporate the weight-lifting portion into an existing body sculpting/bodybuilding routine. The following is a typical routine:

- Monday: forearms and wrists
- Tuesday: arms (biceps/triceps)
- Wednesday: chest
- Thursday: shoulders and back
- Friday: legs and abdomen
- Saturday: forearms and wrists
- Sunday: rest

This routine serves as an example. Tailor the exercises so they fit your personal routine. The most important thing is to strengthen those parts of the body needed to manipulate the cane effectively.

By strengthening these muscles, you will achieve the desired results. And more importantly, you will not quit in frustration after only a few weeks or months of practice.

Supplement: Cane versus Knife

Introduction

Many martial arts systems claim methods of defense against a knife. If you have ever faced an experienced knife-fighter, then you know that no fancy kick, wrist lock, or takedown will thwart even a poorly executed attack.

What constitutes an experienced knife-fighter? More than likely, it is an individual who has spent time in prison. As a police officer, I have first-hand experience in dealing with such fighters. This section addresses what you and your cane can do to defend against the knife.

Cane Advantages

The cane or walking stick is a perfect weapon for one reason: it is legal to carry anywhere. You can even go through airport security without a raised eyebrow from security. Try walking through a security checkpoint or into a restaurant carrying a pair of nunchaku or sai. Compared to the knife, the cane is considerably longer. Figure 432 shows this singular advantage

Anatomy of a Knife-Fighter

There are basically two types of knife-fighters: amateurs and professionals. Both are deadly. Given cane-fighting skills, you may ward off an amateur's attack and come out alive. Most amateurs will "hack and slash" at you. Thus, you can use the cane's length and your stick-fighting skills to survive.

The cane's shaft can help maintain the distance between a knife-fighter's blade and your body. But, watch your weapon hand!

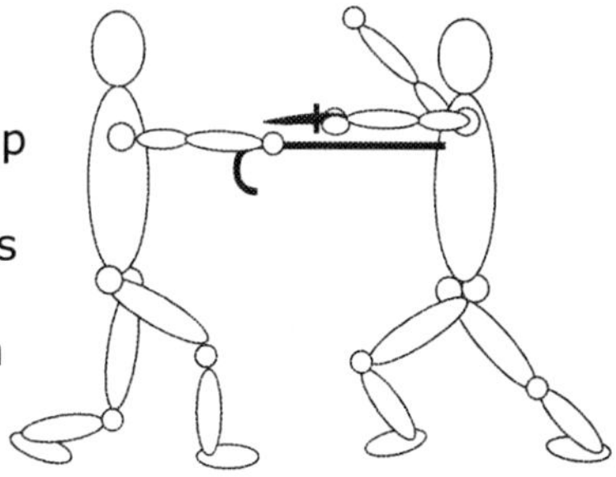

Fig. 432

Professionals have the ability to follow up an initial attack, making them extremely dangerous.

Most effective knife attacks involve stealth. As a result, assassins and military fighters use the knife under surprise conditions. The idea in such attacks is to kill quickly and silently.

Punks and street fighters have taken stealth and pushed it to another level. For example, some conceal the knife (sometimes called "palming" the blade) and strike at the last possible moment. In many instances you just do not have the time to execute a defense.

If you manage to survive an initial surprise attack (or experience a minor wound), the knife-fighter will usually press a secondary attack. Your goal should be to create distance. Use your cane to thrust or strike at the opponent's vital areas then create distance.

The Standoff

If you successfully create distance, an experienced knife-fighter will usually assume a knife-fighting position. Figure 433 shows the most effective knife-fighting stance. This type of stance was originally developed at Folsom prison and most likely was inspired by military knife-fighting stances.

As shown in Fig. 433, the knife-fighter crouches low, holding the knife against his or her body. The free hand is used to jab and distract the defender. If you "bite" when he or she feigns with this hand, you are as good as dead.

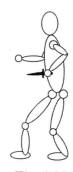

Fig. 433

A knife-fighting stance that means business.

The Jab 'n' Stab

Figures 434 and 435 demonstrate a favored knife-fighting technique known as the jab 'n' stab. In Fig 434, the knife-fighter jabs at the defender, who uses his cane to ward off the attack. In Fig. 435, the knife-fighter closes distance and thrusts with the knife hand. The result is obvious.

Fig. 434

1. Jab: the knife-fighter jabs with his or her free hand. The defender instinctively wards off the attack with a block or strike.

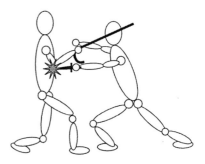

Fig. 435

2. Stab: the knife-fighter moves in and strikes with the blade.

Simple Defense

If you have any alternative, do not use any blocking techniques against a knife. You will lose. The best defense against a knife is an all-out offense. Strike first, often, and hard.

Do not wait for a knife wielder to strike first. As predators, we instinctively respond to movement. By feigning or jabbing, the knife-fighter easily draws you into web, where he or she is in a position to finish you off.

If you do respond to a feint or jab, use the cane's tip to strike hard enough to break bone. Go for body mass, tearing your way up or down as much of it as you can.

Use the Cinco Tiros power strikes both to keep an opponent at bay and to strike at the knife hand or any body part that presents itself, particularly the head or groin. You also could execute a feint of your own, where you begin one technique (Fig. 436) then switch to another (Fig. 437).

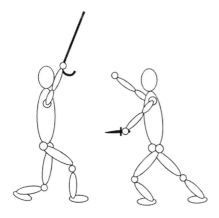

Fig. 436

A feint of your own, as you raise the cane up to draw an opponent inside.

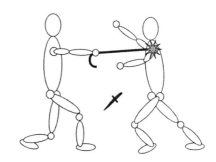

Fig. 437

A quick switch to a thrust to the upper chest could cause the assailant to drop the knife. At the very least, it will cause some discomfort.

A Final Word

No singular text can provide a complete understanding of a particular system or fighting art. The principal purpose of this book has been to give the reader a fundamental understanding of a street-legal self-defense tool. Study the strike and block sets, use the fighting section to integrate them, then create your own techniques. And most importantly, carry your cane everywhere you go. Remember, the cane is only useful if you have it with you.

Peace.

About the Author

Octavio Ramos Jr. served as a Deputy Sheriff for Los Alamos County for five years and was a member of the New Mexico Mounted Patrol, a statewide law-enforcement agency, for more than ten years, during which he was certified in a number of weapons, including pepper spray and the ASP baton, and qualified with firearms every year. His martial arts experience includes Filipino Kali (stick and knife fighting) and Goju-Shorei Karate weapons (cane and knife).

Octavio presently works as a technical writer-editor for Los Alamos National Laboratory. He has published two nonfiction books (*Cerro Grande: Canyons of Fire, Spirit of Community* and *Top Tips to Overcome Diabetes*), several fiction books (*Scout, Smoke Signals, Skull Smasher,* and *Sand Devils*), and several chapbooks (*Folio of Edicts* and *Blood Freaks*). In addition, he has more than 250 publications in magazines, such as *The Police Marksman, Sheriff Times, Police Times, Sounds of Death Magazine, Explicitly Intense, Pit Magazine, The Zone, Double Danger Tales, Bizarre Bazaar, The Silver Web, Best of the Midwest,* and *Showcase.*

LaVergne, TN USA
18 August 2010
193664LV00003B/25/A